DATE DUE

Undergraduate Education in Foreign Affairs

By PERCY W. BIDWELL

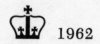 1962

KING'S CROWN PRESS, New York

COPYRIGHT © 1962 COLUMBIA UNIVERSITY PRESS, NEW YORK AND LONDON

LIBRARY OF CONGRESS CATALOG CARD NUMBER: 62-10452

MANUFACTURED IN THE UNITED STATES OF AMERICA

Preface

In the summer of 1958, Carnegie Corporation asked me to undertake an inquiry into undergraduate education in foreign affairs. Originally, the inquiry was intended as a report to the officers of the Corporation. They wanted to know how much and what kind of instruction was being offered college students to give them some sense of the realities of our foreign policy and the nature of world affairs. As the exploration developed and interest grew, it became evident that the report would prove useful to many persons who are concerned with the present state, and future, of higher education in the United States. Consequently, the decision was made to publish the report for wider distribution.

This study deals with the education of the typical American undergraduate in the field of foreign affairs. "Foreign affairs" refers to international relations, cultural and economic as well as political, and particularly to the foreign relations of the United States. "Knowledge of foreign affairs" implies acquaintance with the history, the geography, and the political, social, and economic institutions of the major foreign countries, with their racial characteristics, their cultural achievements, and their religious beliefs. Other surveys have dealt with the preparation of small groups of advanced undergraduates and graduate students for teaching and research, for positions in the Department of State and other federal agencies, on the staff of the United Nations, or in the foreign departments of banks and business corporations. The present study is concerned with general rather than with specialized education. It is focused on the common run of undergraduates—young men and women who are looking forward to careers in teaching, business, engineering, law, medicine, or in some other profession.

Other studies have included in their scope extracurricular activities, community programs and other types of adult education. This study is restricted to work in formal courses at the undergraduate level, in four-year institutions of higher learning—colleges, universities, technical institutes, and teachers colleges. Junior colleges are not included. These important newcomers to the field of higher education, which now enroll over 500,000 young men and women, have failed to develop innovations which are significant for the purposes of this study. Their general education courses closely resemble those offered in the four-year institutions to which many of their students hope to transfer.

Because little work has previously been done in the field, published material is scarce, except for a few articles in learned journals. Directories, issued by the U.S. Office of Education and by private agencies, and college catalogs proved helpful in selecting representative institutions. College catalogs list the titles of many courses which deal, directly or indirectly, with foreign affairs, but they rarely provide accurate, detailed descriptions of the content of these courses. To obtain this information, I interviewed faculty members and administrators in some 40 colleges and universities. I also addressed questionnaires to academic deans and heads of departments in 226 representative institutions, asking their opinions on the most effective ways of improving the average undergraduate's education in foreign affairs. The 200 replies which I received, and the ensuing correspondence, made valuable contributions to the study.

To get an approximate measure of how much the non-specialist undergraduate knows about foreign affairs, an 80-question test was given in May–June, 1960, to some 1,900 students selected at random from the senior classes at 175 colleges and universities across the country. Information on enrollments in undergraduate courses dealing with foreign affairs was obtained by analysis of the academic records of about 1,600 seniors selected at random from 36 colleges and universities.

I thankfully acknowledge the help received from college presidents, deans, and professors, who found time in their busy lives to supply information and advice in interviews and correspondence. To Robert Solomon, of the Educational Testing Service, and to Judith Malkiel, his assistant, thanks are due for preparing the Test on Foreign Affairs and for analyzing the results. (Appendix A incorporates substantial parts of their report on the Test.) I have profited from the comments of the following scholars who read the manuscript, either in part or as a whole: Frederick Burkhardt, George Soule, Richard N. Swift, Lawrence H. Chamberlain, John C. Campbell, Kingsley Davis, Douglas Dunham, K. William Kapp, Julius W. Pratt, and William T. Ross.

Earl J. McGrath gave wise counsel at various stages of the study. Thanks are due to Kenneth Toepfer, who worked with me as research assistant for several months, and to Irwin Oder and Herman Kauz who were similarly employed for shorter periods.

The graphs reproduced are the work of E. D. Weldon. William D. Schlutow, Jr. prepared the map. He used an outline map published by the American Map Company which kindly gave permission to reproduce it. Maria Birnbaum typed some of the manuscript. My principal helper throughout the study was Lorraine Parsont. The book owes much to her competent services as secretary and research assistant, and to her devotion to the task.

To the Carnegie Corporation I am grateful for suggesting that I undertake the study, and for financing it.

In this, as in previous enterprises, I have profited greatly from my wife's encouragement and criticism.

PERCY W. BIDWELL

New York
July, 1961

Contents

FIGURES

TABLES

1. The Problem

The adjustment of American education, at the undergraduate level, to the rapidly changing international scene is the problem examined in this study. In the years 1955 to 1960, twenty-nine new nations in Africa and Asia, formerly dependencies of European states, achieved the status of independent political units. Their appearance in the international arena has created new problems in American foreign policy and has rendered old problems more difficult. At the same time, in countries which long ago obtained independence, internal disturbances have threatened traditional relations with the United States. Sharpened Russian competition in scientific progress, in military power, and in the arts of diplomacy has threatened the prestige of the United States and its leadership in the Western world. These new developments, added to conflicts with the USSR dating from the end of World War II, have created for the United States "a condition of constant peril."

The times require ". . . a public understanding, at once subtle, compassionate, and widespread, of the relationship of the United States to other nations."[1] Rapid strides in communications have multiplied our contacts with foreign countries,

enlarging the area of possible conflict as well as of cooperation. And now, owing to the destructive capacity of new weapons, international conflicts threaten the extinction of great
masses of people, some say all people. The pace of technical
and social change all over the world is quickening. Under these
conditions, decisions of American foreign policy are freighted
with vast consequences.

The Constitution places primary responsibility for the conduct of relations with foreign countries on the President. But,
over the years, Congress has exercised increasing influence in
this domain; the Senate through its power to withhold con-
firmation of appointments and ratification of treaties, and the
House through its control of the purse. Both legislative bodies,
as well as the President, are sensitive to public opinion, particularly when it exerts pressure through tightly organized
groups. Such pressure, when based on prejudice and ignorance
rather than on wise interpretation of significant facts, may prevent the President from acting constructively in the national
interest.

Today, as never before, the American people are participating, indirectly but nevertheless importantly, in the making of
foreign policy. They cannot initiate policy but they may, in
effect, through expressions of disapproval, veto proposed new
measures or cause established policies to be modified or aban-
doned. Yet great numbers of voters lack the knowledge and
understanding of foreign countries and international relations,
which are essential to intelligent, responsible judgments. This
grave weakness in our democracy challenges American education at all levels, from the elementary grades to the universities.

President, then Senator, Kennedy once remarked, "I do not
know whether the Battle of Waterloo was actually won on the
playing fields of Eton. But it is no exaggeration to say that the

struggle in which we are now engaged may well be won or lost in the classrooms of America."[2] In this study, we are concerned with what typical undergraduates are learning, or failing to learn, about foreign affairs in the classrooms of American colleges and universities. In their future careers, they will have little use for specialized knowledge of international relations. As American citizens, however, they will participate in making foreign policy. Periodically, in voting for a president, a senator, or a congressman, they, in effect, will be supporting the type of foreign policy for which the candidate stands. Moreover, their civic responsibility will not be discharged merely on election days. In every American community, college graduates form the group that supplies community leaders. On all questions of public affairs, including foreign affairs, their opinions carry weight with their friends and acquaintances. The wider their knowledge of the international scene, the higher is the probability that their judgments will be sound.

A liberal education is rated high by students, their parents, and their instructors among the benefits to be obtained from "going to college." But a liberal education is incomplete without something more than a passing acquaintance with the world outside the United States. For the college graduate's full enjoyment of his physical and cultural environment, for the satisfaction of his intellectual curiosity, and for the full development of his mental capacities, he needs knowledge and understanding of foreign countries. He ought to be acquainted with the distinctive features of their topography, their climate, their natural resources, and their principal industries. He needs to be informed about the operation of their political institutions. He needs to recognize and appreciate their cultural achievements.

College graduates of this generation who least expect it

may eventually find themselves at work abroad. For there is a growing demand in staffing our multifarious foreign operations for "amateurs," well-educated men and women distinguished more for their good judgment, their intelligence, and their integrity than for expertise in foreign affairs. Yet the run-of-the-mine college graduate is ill-prepared for this type of work in either public or private employment. In language skills, he is particularly deficient. Only a few recent graduates can correctly translate into English simple prose written in a foreign language; even fewer can speak or understand it when it is spoken. Many are deficient in "cultural empathy." They are unable rapidly to acquire an understanding and an appreciation of a foreign civilization or feel at ease in a foreign environment.

John Dewey, it has been said, " . . . directed his revolt not against tradition, but against a rather recent development—the gap created by the inability of Americans to adjust their conceptions of education and culture to the terms of the changing world about them."[3] The opinion is widespread that in the field of foreign affairs American colleges, in general, have not done a good job for the common run of undergraduate, either in preparing him for his civic responsibilities, or for possible service abroad, or in equipping him with the knowledge and understanding of foreign countries which are the hallmarks of a liberal education. Higher education in the United States, we are told on good authority, is more provincial than that of any comparable country. Seniors emerge from our colleges and universities with little more acquaintance with foreign affairs than when they entered as freshmen. Well-informed observers have stated that American colleges and universities do not "produce graduates who are adequately informed, interested, realistic, sensitive, and responsible so far as events and conditions outside the United States are concerned."[4]

As a rough measure of what the typical college senior knows about foreign affairs a test was given in May–June, 1960, to some two thousand seniors selected at random[5] at 36 colleges and universities across the country. The questions were designed to test students' knowledge and understanding of significant facts in the history, geography, and political institutions of foreign countries, and American policy and international relations. The omission of questions in the fields of sociology and anthropology was not owing to failure to recognize their significance in international relations but rather because of the practical need of restricting the scope of the examination.

The test, which was prepared by the Educational Testing Service on the basis of suggestions from over 100 persons with experience in foreign affairs and public affairs in general, is reproduced in Appendix A with critical analysis of the scores. In the author's opinion, these scores confirm the general statements quoted above regarding the typical undergraduate's ignorance of foreign affairs. The test also revealed interesting differences among students in various curricula, types of institutions, and geographical regions.

The average undergraduate's lack of knowledge of foreign affairs, as revealed by the Test on Foreign Affairs, is symptomatic of a more general and widespread weakness in American higher education. A similar test in other fields—in chemistry, physics, mathematics, literature, or philosophy—would also disclose disturbing deficiencies. These deficiencies, particularly in the natural sciences, have been recognized and are now receiving attention. But ignorance of foreign affairs, on the part of several hundred thousand young men and women

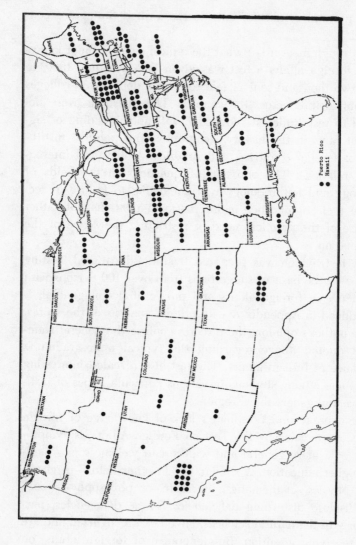

Fig. 1. Distribution of colleges and universities from which information was obtained for this study

who each year join the ranks of so-called educated citizens, a dangerous deficiency in the present crisis in American foreign relations, has received hardly any attention and practically no remedial action.

A senior's lack of knowledge of foreign affairs should not be ascribed solely to defects·in his college education. He may have come from a home, and a community, whose members were concerned exclusively with local and domestic matters. His elementary and secondary schools may have failed to give him an adequate preparation in history, geography, and modern languages. Thus, he may have entered college with little knowledge of countries outside the United States and little curiosity about them.

During his four years at college, he will not lack opportunities to outgrow these deficiencies. College curricula display an abundance of specialized courses dealing with international relations, American foreign policy, and the history of foreign countries—their political and economic institutions and their social and cultural life. It is true that these courses refer principally to the countries of Western Europe, but this deficiency is now being rapidly repaired by the addition of new courses on the so-called non-Western areas, the Far East, Africa, Latin America, the USSR, and Eastern Europe.

But specialized courses which are concerned with foreign countries and international relations enroll only a small fraction of the total undergraduate body. (See Chapter 2.) Few of them are required for the Bachelor's degree; they are not popular as electives since to most students they appear to have no vocational value.

Major traffic points in the undergraduate curriculum are the introductory courses in history, government, economics, sociology, and anthropology. These general education courses, as we shall show in Chapter 3, concentrate their attention on the American scene, neglecting valuable opportunities to deepen the students' understanding of American institutions by comparison and contrast with those of foreign countries.

Largely on account of graduation requirements, students flock in large numbers to beginning courses in English literature and modern languages. In most colleges these courses fail to contribute as much as they might to students' understanding of contemporary social life and the cultural achievements of Britain, France, Germany, and other Western European countries. Few students engage in the study of non-Western languages and literatures.

In general, the chances are rather small that the run-of-the-mine undergraduate will become better acquainted, *in formal courses,* with the history, the politics, or the social and cultural life of foreign countries. As a freshman or sophomore, prerequisite requirements and other college regulations, plus his own lack of interest, prevent his taking the specialized courses which would afford this sort of knowledge, and in these years, his general education courses fail to supply it. In his junior and senior years, he will be too much absorbed in preparing for a career in business, teaching, engineering, or some other profession to choose electives in fields remote from his vocational interests.

In this rather dim picture, a few bright spots appear. In some universities, freshmen and sophomores are being taught American history as a part of world history. One can find courses in introductory sociology which are designed to reveal to the students what is general or universal in human society, so that through contrasts with foreign institutions they may gain insight into those of their own country. Some teachers of introductory government courses are devoting substantial

attention to American foreign policy and international relations. In elementary economics, new courses built around the
concept of economic development introduce the student immediately to problems of foreign trade and investment. International relations, a subject previously reserved for upperclassmen most of whom were intending to specialize in foreign
affairs, now in an increasing number of colleges is taught to
freshmen and sophomores, as part of their general education.
Teachers of English literature and world literature are recognizing that their introductory courses may serve as gateways
to understanding foreign cultures. Along with the postwar
revival in the study of French, German, and Spanish, have
come revolutionary changes in the methods and the goals of
instruction in modern languages. Significant innovations in
this field have enlarged the undergraduates' knowledge of
foreign countries, particularly those of Western Europe.

These are advances in the right direction, but in most colleges and universities they have not gone far enough. The
following chapters will continue to analyze the present situation and will present recommendations for further improvement. They will raise and attempt to answer questions such
as these:

Why do so many specialized courses in the history, the
geography, the economic and social institutions of foreign
countries attract so few students?

Is it possible to revise the content of general education
courses, making them more effective in providing knowledge
and understanding of foreign countries and at the same time
deepening students' understanding and appreciation of the
history and the institutions of their own country?

The information about foreign countries and the problems
of international relations which students derive from general

education courses, even after revision, will usually be frag-
mentary and disjointed. How can scattered facts and flashes
of understanding be coordinated and interrelated? Can this
best be accomplished by requiring all undergraduates to take
a course in international relations, or in world issues, or American foreign policy? Or must each student integrate his own
knowledge of the international scene?

What importance should be attached to extracurricular activities, such as lectures by visiting foreign diplomats and State
Department experts? What educational value for foreign
affairs have exhibitions of the work of foreign artists, concerts
by distinguished musicians from abroad, undergraduate programs of foreign travel and study?

Can extracurricular activities be effective in stimulating student interest in foreign affairs, in creating a new climate of
campus opinion, in supplementing work in formal courses?

What would be the most effective means of mobilizing and
coordinating a university's varied and scattered resources, curricular and extracurricular, in all schools and divisions, for
undergraduate education in foreign affairs?

2. Neglected Opportunities

Catalogs of state and private universities display a rich intellectual menu in the field of foreign affairs, and independent liberal arts colleges, considering their more limited resources, make an impressive showing. Some technical institutes offer a dozen or more courses which provide information about foreign countries. But anyone who attempted to measure the undergraduates' exposure to foreign affairs, in any college, by a tally of relevant, or apparently relevant, courses listed in its annual catalog, could go far astray. Some courses are given either in alternate years, or irregularly. Quite frequently, an inactive course will have been carried in the catalog for several years before being dropped for lack of student interest. Although descriptions of courses are significant as statements of desires and aspirations, they rarely provide full and accurate accounts of what is being taught. A further deficiency in the catalogs, from the point of view of this study, is that they furnish no information on the numbers of students enrolled in each course.

Information supplied by registrars and other college officers shows that small enrollments, composed principally of majors in the field, are typical of upper division courses. Some illustrative figures, *referring only to courses dealing directly with some aspect of foreign affairs,* are given below:

At Macalester, a liberal arts college in St. Paul, Minnesota, (with a total undergraduate enrollment of 1,500) in the second semester 1958–59, enrollments in six specialized courses were:

American Diplomatic History	24
History of the Middle East	18
International Economics	16
International Organization	12
Far Eastern Government and Politics	11
Far East Area Study	10

At Hunter College, in New York City, with 6 thousand full-time undergraduates in the day sessions, enrollments in the fall semester 1959–60, in nine upper division courses dealing with foreign countries were:

History of Russia	39
Communism in Eastern Europe	37
Political Emergence of Africa	35
Dynamics of German Politics	28
Comparative Economic Systems	22
United Nations	21
International Politics	20
Comparative Societies	20
International Trade	11

At Michigan State University (East Lansing), an institution with 15,900 undergraduates, 24 upper division courses in the general field of foreign affairs had 665 students in October 1959. Included were 12 courses in political science with a total enrollment of 361 students.[1]

The number of students who, at the beginning of a semester,

sign up for any course depends largely on college regulations,—whether or not it is required as a condition for graduation, or as one of the components of a major program. (See the discussion of distribution and concentration in Chapter 9.) All college curricula provide an area of elective courses, in which students may choose what they will study. However, their choice is not entirely free. Often juniors and seniors are unable to register in an upper division course because in their first and second years they had not taken prerequisite courses. We shall not attempt to analyze all of the circumstances, relevant and irrelevant, which determine students' choices. The time of day at which the course is given may be decisive, or the day of the week—Saturday courses are notoriously unpopular. General undergraduate opinion—is the subject dull or interesting, does the professor know his stuff, is he a hard marker—has much weight. The "dope" on a course usually circulates by word of mouth. The situation at Harvard is exceptional: the undergraduate daily, *The Crimson,* publishes each year, for the benefit of freshmen, a *Confidential Guide to Lower Level Courses* which provides responsible comment on the content of courses and on the instructors.

Serious students who want to make the best use of their educational opportunities will rely on the advice of their counsellors or other faculty members. Young men and women who are intent upon fitting themselves for a job, the most numerous group in any college, will probably choose as electives courses as closely related to their major programs as the regulations permit. Thus, political science majors tend to choose as electives courses in some other department of the social science division, and mathematics majors will take the bulk of their electives in the natural science division.

Estimates of Exposure

College deans and faculty members across the country have reported, in letters to the author, that a substantial number of their students emerge from four years of college without having had more than a minimum exposure, in formal courses, to knowledge and understanding of foreign countries. Dean Riley of the University of Washington writes:

I made an actual count of the 1958 and 1959 graduating class in the College of Arts and Sciences and discovered that 30% of the entire class (each year) had not had a course or courses introducing comparative data on foreign countries and foreign areas.

The results of his calculations agree with the estimate of Professor C. P. Edwards of Westminster College (Pennsylvania):

I would guess that at least a third of the student body are at present able to meet all college requirements *without* taking any courses that concern foreign countries.

From the University of South Carolina, Dean Wienefeld writes:

We feel that we are introducing the world at large to about one-half of our student body in the first year and attracting a substantial number in the sophomore year.

Instructors in the Department of History at Columbia University estimate that somewhat less than half the undergraduates at that institution enroll in courses in which they might acquire knowledge and understanding of foreign countries. From 50 to 55 percent of the class graduating at Hamilton College each year, a faculty member estimates, will have had no formal course work in foreign affairs.

The foregoing estimates, it should be noted, come from liberal arts colleges, either independent or related to universities. In the professional schools, the proportion of students having had no exposure to the international scene is much higher,

owing partly to the pressure of required work in technical subjects and partly to students' preferences. Dean Bear of the
College of Sciences and Humanities at Iowa State University
writes that in his institution, as in most scientific and technical
schools,

. . . the pressures of professional programs would at present make
it difficult for any students but those choosing to specialize in
foreign cultures to learn much about this except in a small and
almost accidental way. The students majoring in the sciences and
humanities here are required to expose themselves for about one-
fourth of their baccalaureate programs to courses in the areas of
economics, sociology, psychology, government, history, literature,
philosophy and modern languages, but there is considerable freedom
of choice and no guarantee that foreign cultures will be adequately
covered in a given selection.

Similar comment has been received from Rensselaer Poly-
technic Institute, where a new School of Humanities and Social
Sciences was recently established. Dean Mueller writes that
the opportunities thus afforded R.P.I. students to enlarge their
knowledge of the world outside the United States are restricted to relatively few students: "The limited time available
to students in Engineering and Science Curricula does not
make it possible for them to choose such courses in great
numbers."

To supplement the foregoing general observations, and to
test their accuracy, we examined the transcripts of academic
records of 1,645 seniors in 36 representative colleges and universities:

State Universities: University of Alabama, University of Arizona,
University of California (Los Angeles), Indiana University, Uni-
versity of Kansas, University of Maryland, University of Minnesota,
University of North Carolina, Pennsylvania State University
Private Universities: Columbia University, Stanford University, Yale
University

Liberal Arts Colleges: Augustana (South Dakota), Berea, Birmingham-Southern, Carleton, Colby, Colgate University, Colorado College, Denison, Hollins, Hunter College of the City of New York, Oberlin, Pomona, Reed, St. Mary's University of San Antonio, Wellesley, Wittenberg

Teachers Colleges: Colorado State College, Teachers College of Connecticut (New Britain), Kansas State Teachers College, State University of New York College of Education at New Paltz

Technical Schools: California Institute of Technology, Carnegie Institute of Technology, Case Institute of Technology

Each institution supplied a sample, selected at random from the transcripts of academic records of students receiving their B.A. or first professional degree either in June, 1958, or June, 1959. In most instances, the sample ranged from 4 to 10 percent of the graduating class. From the catalog of each of the institutions in our sample, we selected the courses which appeared to have as a major purpose instruction in some aspect of foreign affairs, e.g., a course in the history of Russia, or a course in the geography of Africa. These we called *Direct Exposure* courses. Courses which provided knowledge of foreign affairs only marginally or incidentally we put in a second group, labeled *Indirect Exposure*. Examples are an introductory course in government, or in sociology.

The Direct Exposure group comprises courses in which upperclassmen are principally enrolled; Indirect Exposure courses are usually taken in the freshman and sophomore years. However, courses in Western civilization which we have listed as Direct Exposure, and introductory courses in geography, are usually taught in the lower division. Except for Western civilization, Direct Exposure courses are rarely required for graduation. They are chosen for the most part by liberal arts students concentrating in international relations, history, politics, or economics.

Classification of the transcripts according to semester hours of Direct Exposure showed that almost 20 percent of the seniors had not taken, during their four years of college, any course which provided knowledge of foreign affairs in substantial measure. (See Table 1.) The modal group, 21.9 percent of the total number of students, showed 4–6 semester hours of Direct Exposure, or 3–5 percent of the total of 120 semester hours usually required for graduation. On the bulk of the transcripts, 73 percent of the total, courses having direct relevance to foreign affairs totaled less than 10 semester hours.

Analysis of the transcripts according to the students' fields of specialization or concentration[2] shows that all but 1.8 percent of 274 social science majors had taken, during their four years, at least one course which provided substantial information about foreign affairs. (See Table 2 and Figures 2, 3, and 4.) The modal exposure group had 10–12 semester hours. Students majoring in the natural sciences or the humanities,

Table 1. DIRECT EXPOSURE COURSES

Transcripts showing:	Number of Transcripts	Percent of Total
0 exposure	309	18.8
1–3 hours	286	17.4
4–6 hours	359	21.9
7–9 hours	253	15.4
10–12 hours	129	7.8
13–15 hours	88	5.3
16–18 hours	63	3.8
19–21 hours	46	2.8
22–24 hours	30	1.8
25–27 hours	28	1.7
More than 27 hours	54	3.3
Total	1,645	100.0

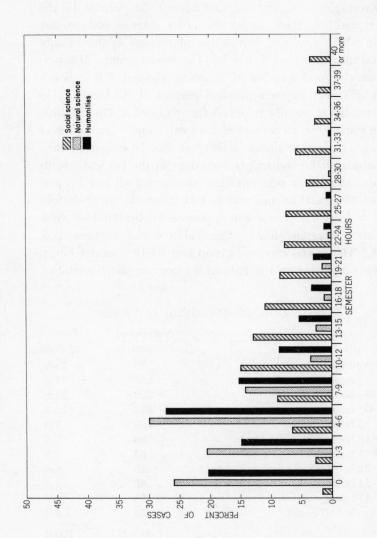

Fig. 2. Distribution of direct exposure, students in social science, natural science, and humanities

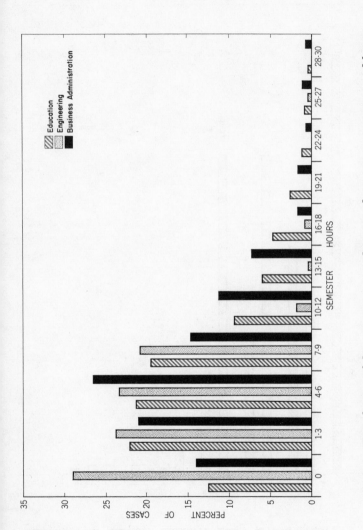

Fig. 3. Distribution of direct exposure, students in education, engineering, and business administration

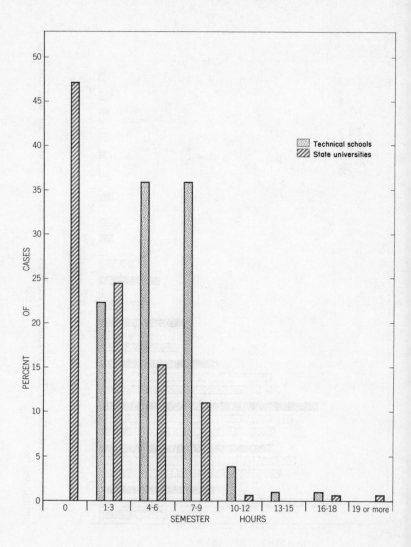

Fig. 4. Distribution of direct exposure, students in engineering

judging from their transcripts, showed much less interest in the international scene. Business administration students were on a par, in this respect, with majors in the natural sciences and the humanities. Engineering students (in universities) and young men and women preparing to be teachers, ranked lowest in Direct Exposure courses.

Only 20 percent of the transcripts of the social science majors showed less than 10 semester hours in courses directly related to foreign affairs. But in education, 75 percent of the transcripts showed less than 10 hours; in business administration, 76 percent; in the humanities, 77 percent; in the natural sciences, 90 percent; engineers in state universities, 98 percent; and engineers in technical schools, 94 percent.

Judging from their transcripts, students concentrating in history and government showed much more interest in foreign affairs than those specializing in economics and sociology. The average Direct Exposure of students in these subgroups was:

Government	21.9 hours
History	21.7 hours
Economics	14.5 hours
Sociology-anthropology	10.2 hours

Our sample of students specializing in engineering included students enrolled in departments of engineering in state universities and students in independent engineering schools. Every one of the 103 transcripts obtained from the latter showed some Direct Exposure and 72 percent had 4–9 hours. But, of the 163 transcripts obtained from state universities, 47 percent showed no Direct Exposure and only 26 percent showed 4–9 hours. The contrast is owing largely to the fact that Western civilization is a required course in the technical schools represented in our sample.

To identify the *courses* which constituted Direct Exposure,

Table 2. DISTRIBUTION OF DIRECT EXPOSURE, BY FIELDS OF CONCENTRATION

(Percent of students in each exposure interval)[a]

Direct Exposure in Semester Hours	Social Sciences (274)[b]	Natural Sciences (254)[b]	Humanities (243)[b]	Education (344)[b]	Engineering		Business Administration (178)[b]	Miscellaneous[c] (86)[b]	Total (1645)[b]
					Technical Schools (103)[b]	Technical Universities (163)[b]			
0	1.8	26.0	20.2	12.5	—	47.2	14.0	51.2	18.8
1–3	2.6	20.5	14.8	22.1	22.3	24.5	20.8	17.4	17.4
4–6	6.6	29.9	27.2	21.2	35.9	15.3	26.4	19.8	21.9
7–9	8.8	14.2	15.2	19.5	35.9	11.0	14.6	9.3	15.4
10–12	15.0	3.5	8.6	9.3	3.9	0.6	11.2	1.2	7.8
13–15	12.8	2.4	5.3	5.8	1.0	—	7.3	—	5.3
16–18	10.9	1.2	3.3	4.7	1.0	0.6	1.7	1.2	3.8
19–21	8.4	1.6	2.9	2.6	—	—	1.7	—	2.8
22–24	7.7	0.4	1.2	1.2	—	0.6	0.6	—	1.8
25–27	7.3	—	0.8	0.9	—	—	1.1	—	1.7
28–30	4.0	0.4	—	0.3	—	0.6	0.6	—	0.9
31–33	5.8	—	0.4	—	—	—	—	—	1.0
34 or more	8.4	—	—	—	—	—	—	—	1.4

a Percentages may not add to 100.0 due to decimal places. Note that percentages are to be added vertically.

b Figures in parentheses represent number of transcripts in field of concentration.

c Includes agriculture, architecture, home economics, law, medicine, nursing, pharmacy.

we examined the records of students who made up the modal groups in each field of concentration. In natural sciences, 76 transcripts showed 4–6 semester hours of Direct Exposure. On 38 of these transcripts, we find a course in Western civilization; on 7, a course in history of a foreign country or region; and on 7, a course in geography. The same pattern appears on transcripts of the modal groups in the humanities. In education and in engineering, the typical Direct Exposure (1–3 semester hours) is made up of either a general education course in Western civilization or a course in geography. Among the modal group in business administration, geography—principally economic geography—appears most frequently, with Western civilization in second place. (See Table 3.)

Table 3. DIRECT EXPOSURE COURSES APPEARING
MOST FREQUENTLY ON TRANSCRIPTS IN
MODAL GROUPS

Field of Concentration	Western Civilization	History	Geography
	(Number of transcripts)		
Natural Science	38	7	7
Humanities	31	14	17
Education	39	5	17
Engineering	33	0	8
Business Administration	21	5	36

INDIRECT EXPOSURE

In addition to Direct Exposure courses, usually taught in the upper division, all transcripts showed enrollment in one or more general or survey courses which dealt marginally, or peripherally, with foreign countries or with United States foreign policy. These we have classified as Indirect Exposure courses. Table 4, Distribution of Indirect Exposure, by Fields of Concentration, shows that the modal Indirect Exposure for the 1,645 transcripts was 4–6 hours; 68 percent showed less than 10 hours. In two fields—natural science and humanities —the modal Indirect Exposure is the same as in Direct Exposure courses, viz., 4–6 hours. The transcripts of engineers showed the fewest hours of Indirect Exposure; social science majors had the most, 10–12 hours. In general, the scores in Indirect Exposure courses emphasized the *differences* in attention to foreign affairs between the social science majors and students specializing in other fields. Business administration was exceptional. The high modal score in Indirect Exposure of students in this field, 10–12 hours, results from requirements of many schools of business administration that all students take courses in elementary economics and, in some cases, American history as well.

Table 4. DISTRIBUTION OF INDIRECT EXPOSURE, BY FIELDS OF CONCENTRATION

(Percent of students in each exposure interval)[a]

Indirect Exposure in Semester Hours	Social Sciences (274)[b]	Natural Sciences (254)[b]	Humanities (243)[b]	Education (344)[b]	Engineering		Business Administration (178)[b]	Miscellaneous[c] (86)[b]	Total (1645)[b]
					Technical Schools (103)[b]	Universities (163)[b]			
0	1.5	14.2	19.3	18.0	24.3	12.9	—	8.1	12.3
1–3	7.7	14.6	15.2	21.8	28.2	42.9	1.7	19.8	17.6
4–6	11.7	26.0	22.6	25.0	13.6	28.8	4.5	26.7	20.0
7–9	13.5	21.3	18.9	16.3	29.1	15.3	18.0	26.7	18.4
10–12	23.0	13.0	15.6	10.8	4.9	—	37.6	11.6	15.4
13–15	18.6	7.1	4.9	5.8	—	—	28.1	3.5	9.4
16–18	14.6	3.1	2.1	2.0	—	—	7.9	2.3	4.6
19–21	5.1	0.8	0.4	0.3	—	—	1.1	1.2	1.3
22 or more	4.4	—	0.8	—	—	—	1.1	—	1.0

[a] Percentages may not add to 100.0 due to rounding of decimal places. Note that percentages are to be added vertically.

[b] Figures in parentheses represent number of transcripts in field of concentration.

[c] Includes agriculture, architecture, home economics, law, medicine, nursing, pharmacy.

3. Foreign Affairs in General Education

Only a small proportion of the undergraduate body in any university, we learned in the previous chapter, takes advantage of the opportunities afforded by specialized courses to learn about foreign affairs. About a fifth of a graduating class, according to our analysis of transcripts of academic records, do not enroll in courses of this sort. Undergraduates whose records show exposure to courses which deal with foreign affairs, broadly defined, devote only a small fraction of their college programs to such courses. This chapter examines the content of general education courses, the chief traffic points in the undergraduate curriculum, to find out what they contribute to students' knowledge of foreign affairs.

The general education movement of the past half-century represents a reaction against the disintegrating influence of free electives, and an attempt to introduce, or reintroduce, a greater measure of unity into American higher education. Columbia College, in 1919, led the way with its interdisciplinary program in Contemporary Civilization. The program, which has served as the inspiration and the model for many others, was the outgrowth of a war issues course directed toward explaining the origins of World War I.

World War II gave renewed impetus to general education. "The crucial task of higher education today," said the President's Commission in its 1948 report, ". . . is to provide a unified general education for American youth. Colleges must find the right relationship between specialized training on the one hand, aiming at a thousand different careers, and the transmission of a common cultural heritage toward a common citizenship on the other."[1] Animated by these ideas, and by those expressed in an earlier report of the Harvard Committee on the Objectives of a General Education in a Free Society, some of the larger institutions, notably Harvard and M.I.T., introduced sequences of courses which aimed to give all students a common understanding of the major fields of human knowledge. The University of Chicago, Boston University, and a few other institutions set up, alongside traditional curricula, four-year programs of general education. But in this form the movement has not made substantial progress. At Boston, the General College has been merged with the College of Liberal Arts and will eventually disappear. Since 1958, the University of Chicago's separate enterprise in general education, the College of the University, has been combined with a larger four-year college which includes parts of the various departments of the University. The bachelor's degree, previously awarded for completion of general education requirements alone, now requires, in addition, work in specialized studies. There remains at Chicago, however, a common curriculum and a distinct staff devoted to general education.[2]

To provide the background of general education which, it is assumed, all undergraduates should possess, two types of courses are employed: (1) introductory courses in a single discipline, e.g., a beginning course in government, and (2) interdisciplinary courses such as a course in the history of Western civilization or an integrated social science course.

INTEGRATED SOCIAL SCIENCE

Integrated social science courses, presenting in a single package guiding principles and pertinent data from American history, political science, economics, sociology and social psychology were found, in a 1954 survey by the United States Office of Education, in about 10 percent of all institutions of higher learning.

At Brooklyn College, Social Science 1,2, Our Contemporary World, enrolls about one-half the freshman class. The teaching staff of 35 is taken from the Departments of Economics, Political Science, History, Philosophy, Education, Sociology and Anthropology, and Psychology. In the spring semester of 1959, the course introduced the students to topics usually treated in elementary sociology—the concepts of culture, social structure, social stratification, and the loci of social power. Then followed readings and lectures on "American Social Structure: Character and Development." Under this general heading, were covered American political and economic development and contemporary problems of government and economics. A third major division of the course dealt with the psychology of the individual. Up to this point, emphasis is on American conditions and institutions. International relations, the subject considered in the last three weeks, does not appear closely related to what has preceded.

Emphasis on the American scene is paramount in the required integrated course, Modern Society, taught at Chatham College. At the University of Pittsburgh, the one-year course called Introduction to the Social Sciences devotes one week in the second semester to the comparison of the economic systems of the United States, the Soviet Union, China, and the United Kingdom, and a second week—the last of the term—to American international relations.

American Institutions is the title of a composite course which each year enrolls 3,000 undergraduates at the University of Florida. Assigned readings (no textbook is used) contain materials on anthropology, sociology, government, economics and the political history of Europe, American economic history, and United States foreign relations. In a course of this size, with a teaching staff of almost 100, the emphasis given to foreign affairs in classroom discussions will, of course, vary widely according to the interests and experience of individual instructors.

In engineering and technical schools, in which only limited time is available for liberal arts studies, integrated courses that cut across conventional disciplines are often found. For example, Case Institute of Technology requires all freshmen to enroll in a two-semester course, Social Science, which surveys "the basic concepts in the fields of cultural anthropology, social psychology, sociology, economics and political science." Descriptive materials are drawn mainly, but not exclusively, from the American scene.

Occasionally, one finds integrated courses which give more attention to foreign affairs. Washington State College offers such a course in which approximately one-third of the readings deal with foreign affairs. At the University of Chicago, the course, The Development and Progress of American Democracy, the first in a two-year sequence of general education courses in the social sciences, is concerned with American political and economic history, economic and political theory, and problems in the relation of government to business in the

United States. Readings assigned in the following year's course, Interrelations of Culture and Personality, describe problems of nineteenth-century industrial society, throwing light on European conditions. Topics appearing later include the conflict of ideologies and national interests leading to the participation of the United States in World War II. The final weeks of the course are devoted to comparisons of American culture and institutions with those of the USSR. Altogether, about one-third of the readings and discussions in the second year deal with international affairs. At Michigan State University (East Lansing), a required social science program which now enrolls 4,000 students has been in operation for almost 20 years. In this program, the "international flavor" has recently been strengthened.

Many, perhaps most, educators view with scepticism all attempts to integrate the social sciences in a beginning course for undergraduates. To interrelate concepts and data in the fields of history and the social sciences so as to achieve an overall view, they believe, is a task for mature scholars. Examination of the integrated courses offered in some colleges, and in some high schools, supports this view. Often they present, in abbreviated or condensed form, material found in elementary textbooks of the separate disciplines. Genuine interrelation and interpretation of the disparate materials seem to have been achieved occasionally by exceptionally gifted instructors who are dedicated to their task and who enjoy firm administrative support.

WESTERN CIVILIZATION

Examination of recent catalogs of 35 representative colleges shows that 28 of them offered a course in Western civilization, contemporary civilization, world civilization, or a similar course. These courses have large enrollments. In 13 of the colleges, all students must successfully complete the course before graduation. In six institutions, the course may be used to fulfill a "distribution requirement." Transcripts of the academic records of 1,211 seniors in the 28 colleges which offered the course show that 737 (61 percent) took it.

The content of the course can be described only in general terms because of wide variations in emphasis from one institution to another, and even among instructors in the same course. A few colleges offer a course in world civilization which gives substantial attention to political and cultural developments in India, China and other non-Western countries. Elsewhere, Western civilization or European civilization accurately describes its geographical scope. Some courses are heavily freighted with economic history; in others, cultural and ideological matters receive most attention; but political history usually supplies the framework. Harvard's course, The Development of Western Civilization, according to *The Crimson*, is ". . . a plain, bricks and mortar history course, a solid introduction to European history from the fall of the Roman Empire to Greta Garbo."[3] At institutions which offer a two-year sequence of interdisciplinary courses—e.g., M.I.T. and Chicago —studies in the field of the humanities may occupy a full year.

Columbia's Contemporary Civilization, since its beginning, has been limited to Western civilization. "Such a limitation was made, not from dim awareness of the Orient . . . nor from perversity and false cultural pride, but because Western society is the society of Western students, and because the number of men available versed in Eastern culture has always been lamentably small."[4] Until recently the course was taught in a two-year sequence, the first year dealing with history and the second with contemporary problems. The second year proved unsatisfactory, however, chiefly because of the difficulty ". . . in finding teachers who could encompass a range of materials so different in content and offering so many problems of conceptualization."[5] Consequently, in the fall of 1961, a new plan was introduced. Sophomores will no longer be required to take the second year, Contemporary Civilization B. Instead they may fulfill the requirement by choosing two semesters from a list of courses including Introduction to the History and Culture of Oriental Societies and new beginning courses in anthropology and economics which are not the standard introductory courses in these disciplines.

The superficial character of many Western civilization courses is a grave defect. Attempting to "cover" a great range of time and space, they skim lightly over vast areas of human activity, often attacking the most profound subjects in slapdash fashion. At the end of the year, faculty members are left frustrated, and students are either bored or bewildered. But this situation is not universal or inevitable. In some courses, a measure of success has been achieved by improved organization, by the introduction of the "bloc and gap" method which explores, in depth, a few well-defined epochs—classical antiquity, the rise of Islam, the Renaissance, modern nationalism, etc. A critical feature is the quality of instruction. To survey in a single year, in many colleges in a single semester, the progress of civilization from ancient times, or even from the end of the Middle Ages, to the close of World War II, requires unusual powers of condensation and generalization. Such powers are possessed only by mature scholars who are also skillful teachers.

Courses in Western civilization, like most educational ventures, fall far short of perfection. It is probably true, however, that they contribute more than any other lower division course to the orientation of the common run of student to the international scene. In the academic experience of many students, Western civilization is the only course which provides, in systematic form, information about foreign countries and insight into their affairs. Sections dealing with European history in the nineteenth and twentieth centuries provide valuable background information which is helpful in understanding contemporary international affairs. Of equal importance, probably, are the portions of the course that introduce the student to the literary masterpieces of foreign countries and to the works of their greatest philosophers. Although such an experience may add little to his store of information about foreign countries, it may significantly modify his attitudes and opinions. (For discussion of the contribution of the humanities, particularly modern languages and literature, to knowledge and understanding of foreign countries, see Chapter 7.) What Professor Cole wrote about the Contemporary Civilization course at Columbia is applicable to many others. Such courses ". . . seek to jar the undergraduate out of provincialism, out of complacency, away from the preconceptions and misconceptions he is heir to and to provide him, not with solutions, but with a multiplicity of questions."[6]

Courses within a Single Discipline

Courses in history provide a necessary background for understanding the contemporary situation in foreign countries and the problems of international relations. "Despite the constant danger that man may misinterpret history, he must contemplate events and movements of the past to understand world affairs today. The study of world affairs in fact is an offshoot of historical studies, so history continues to be one of the fields closest in spirit and content to world affairs. History

provides information and perspective about the various encounters among nations and peoples, the economic and social
factors that have influenced them, the struggle for tolerance
and peace, all of which are the indispensable background for
many contemporary issues."[7]

Departments of history often offer courses in United States
Foreign Policy, United States Foreign Relations, or United
States Diplomatic History, which usually are restricted to
juniors and seniors. Among the infrequent exceptions is the
University of Michigan's Foreign Policy of the United States
which, being designed for non-specialists, is open to sophomores without prerequisites. It enrolls undergraduates from
various professional schools as well as from the College of
Literature, Science and the Arts. At Southwestern at Memphis,
National Security Policy of the United States, open to sophomores, is one of the largest electives in the social science field.

Three history courses frequented principally by lower division students show large enrollments: History of Western
Civilization, European history, and history of the United States.
In most institutions students may offer any of the three as
partial or total fulfillment of social science requirements for
the bachelor's degree.

EUROPEAN HISTORY

Western civilization, an interdisciplinary course, we have
already considered. European history courses which give lower
division students the best background for the understanding
of contemporary foreign affairs, in the Western world, are
Europe Since 1815 and Modern Europe. In a few colleges,
e.g., Princeton and the University of Mississippi, European
history is offered as the introductory course for freshmen or
sophomores. In institutions where American history is not a

required subject, many students, particularly those who have made the best records in secondary schools, often prefer to enroll in the European course. Large enrollments give evidence of its popularity. At Oberlin, 70 percent of the entire student body are regularly exposed to it at some time during their college careers. Enrollments at Yale are 250–325 each year; at the University of Illinois about 300, and at Kansas, about 200. At Penn State and the University of Arizona, they reach 400 and at the University of Minnesota, 1,000.

AMERICAN HISTORY

In two courses in American history at Yale, enrollments in 1958 were 200 and 300; in one course at the University of Pittsburgh, 500–600; at Penn State, 1,000; and at U.C.L.A., 1,500. In part, state laws are responsible for the popularity of this course. In many states, all candidates for certificates, entitling them to teach in public schools must have satisfactorily completed at least one college course in American history. Hence, schools of education uniformly include American history as a requirement for the bachelor's degree. A similar requirement, not based on state laws, is found in other professional schools. Certain state universities apply the requirement to all undergraduates. At the University of Missouri, all candidates for undergraduate degrees must complete a course in American history or in American government. Georgia, Texas, California, and other states have enacted similar legislation, but its effect on enrollments should not be exaggerated. If, as often happens, the legislature does not provide funds and administrative machinery for policing a law of this kind, it becomes a dead letter.

The American history requirement is often evaded. Frequenty, students can satisfy it by passing a not-too-difficult qualification examination. At the University of Georgia, 85 percent of the candidates for the B.A. and first professional degree are exempted by examination from enrollment in the introductory course in American history. At the University of Texas and the University of California, liberal interpretations of the "study American" law permit students to meet their requirements by enrolling in any one of a wide variety of courses. In New York City, the Board of Examiners regards a course in the history of the Western hemisphere as American history, and the New York State Board of Regents, going a step further, accepts courses in American interests in the Far East.

Nevertheless, even in states where the legislation is liberally interpreted, its mere presence on the statute books affects enrollments. Some students, either unfamiliar with the escape hatches or preferring to play it safe, sign up for American history, thus neglecting an opportunity to enlarge their knowledge of the history of foreign countries. A factor of greater importance, however, is the students' lack of interest in anything having to do with foreign countries. (See discussion of students' attitudes, Chapter 10.) Besides, having studied American history repeatedly in elementary and secondary grades, they believe that a college course in that subject would require less effort than European history or history of Western civilization.

THE CONTENT OF THE COURSE. In 1944, a committee, sponsored jointly by the American Historical Association and other organizations, condemned the prevailing nationalist approach to the teaching of American history in schools and colleges. The committee contended that the subject should neither be studied nor taught "in isolation from the more inclusive currents of world history." The history of the United States, the committee stated, cannot be fully understood without knowledge of the history of other countries. But interviews and correspondence with teachers in colleges and universities across the country reveal that, in the beginning course, little progress has been made toward broadening its outlook. Professor Roach of the University of Texas has written, in a letter to the author, that courses in American history and government, at the university level, are usually taught

. . . with no reference to what was or is going on in the rest of the world, and with little or no attempt made to contrast American conditions or problems—and the responses to them—with those of other peoples. This merely reinforces the typical student's view of the uniqueness of the American experience, it exaggerates the American accomplishment, it contributes to the unquestioning and uncritical attitudes which frequently exist where American political institutions and practices are concerned, and—I am convinced— sends very many students away believing that the American people and American nation enjoy some kind of existence in a separate plane of time and space rather than as a part of the human race which has a common origin, evolution, and—one hopes—future.

Allowing for some exaggeration, which Professor Roach himself admits, this seems a fairly accurate description of the content of the typical introductory course in American history. Its emphasis, in the majority of institutions, is on the American scene. It gives little attention to either the influences from the outside which affected this country's development or to the impact of the American experiment on political and social institutions abroad. In treating the colonial period and the Revolutionary War and the early years of the new nation, say until 1815, no textbook can avoid connecting American with European history. But then attention to foreign affairs lapses and is renewed only by the Spanish-American War, and by the events leading up to World War I and World War II. The development of the country in the nineteenth century is treated as if it occurred in a vacuum as far as foreign countries were concerned.

The isolated-America course is typical but not universal. The introductory course at the University of California (Los Angeles campus) devotes unusual attention to United States foreign policy. Elsewhere, a new method of teaching American history, linking it with European history and world history, is making headway. Richard Swift found courses of this sort at the University of Iowa, Iowa State College, Ohio State, and Clark University. To this list should be added Yale, Columbia, Carleton College, Teachers College of Connecticut, and Hunter College in New York City.

The description of the course at Hunter called The Foundations of America, more accurate than many blurbs in college catalogs, reads as follows: "A course to acquaint the student with the European heritage of American civilization, the colonial foundations and early national growth of the United States, and its continuing inter-relationship with European developments."[8] The second semester of this course, The United States in World History, is devoted to: "The development of the American people in the 19th and early 20th centuries, stressing our inter-relations with Europe, the evolution of American patterns of living and ideals, and the adaptation of our basic institutions to changing conditions."[9] Although regarded as fairly difficult, the course is popular with students. About two-thirds of them take this course in preference to a course in European history which also fulfills a social science requirement.

TEXTBOOKS IN AMERICAN HISTORY. Examination of textbooks most frequently used in the beginning course in American history tends to confirm the accuracy of Professor Roach's criticism. Inevitably, between teaching and text there is a close, reciprocal relationship. On the one hand, the author, having in mind maximum adoptions, usually will not depart very far from the prevailing pattern of instruction in the course. Instruction, on the other hand, will conform to the text-book. It is true that particularly competent instructors, well-grounded in their subject, will go their own way with only occasional references to the text; but such persons, unfortunately, do not predominate in the teaching staff of introductory courses, particularly in the larger institutions. Instead, we find mostly graduate assistants and young instructors who, because of their lack of confidence and experience, lean heavily on textbooks.[10] Their suggestions for outside reading are usually disregarded, except by a small number of exceptionally well-motivated students. Others, following the instructors' example, stick to the text. The text is the glue that holds the course together. For the students, it provides their principal reading material, it is a source for reference, and it helps to organize the ideas that they have received from other sources.

In their opening chapters, the half-dozen American history textbooks which supply the bulk of the college market give excellent accounts of the conditions, economic and political, in England and other European countries, that gave rise to the settling of the New World. Colonial history they treat correctly as a phase of the history of Western civilization. They show how the new nation was involved in Anglo-French rivalries in its early years, and how, until about 1815, international relations and questions of foreign policy were matters of prime importance. But then a long gap appears. Foreign affairs are not brought into the foreground again until the concluding chapters which tell the story of America's emergence as a world power and its participation in two world wars.

In the intervening period, 1815–1900, foreign relations are

overshadowed by domestic affairs: westward expansion, the growth of internal trade, the controversy over slavery, the Civil War and Reconstruction, and industrial growth in both the North and the South. Incidents in foreign policy, such as the Monroe Doctrine, the Mexican War, and British near-intervention in the Civil War, are mentioned, usually briefly. But too often the reader gets the impression that for almost a century the United States lived entirely apart from the rest of the world. This, of course, was not true. Although the Americans had achieved political independence, they were still heavily dependent on foreign countries for markets for their exports and for capital for long-term investment.

Moreover, in the realm of literature and the fine arts, Americans drew inspiration continually from English, Continental, and even non-Western sources. Yet textbooks in American History, even the best, do not deal adequately with the continuous cultural contacts between the New World and the Old. It is true that, in chapters devoted to advances in literature, one finds sporadic mention of Emerson's indebtedness to Kant and to Eastern poets and philosophers. Washington Irving, Cooper, and Longfellow all profited, we are told, from residence in Europe. Darwinism, imported from England, and the Higher Criticism, from Germany, caused profound disturbances in American religious thought. In education, after the Civil War, important new developments were brought about by Americans trained abroad. All, or most, of these facts one may discover by diligent search in the leading texts but none of them presents, in orderly fashion, a systematic account of the foreign influences that helped to mould the intellectual and artistic life of the new nation. American cultural development, consequently, appears as an isolated phenomenon rather than in its true guise as an offshoot of European culture.

Textbook writers, in giving their readers the impression that foreign affairs were unimportant in American history throughout most of the nineteenth century, seem to have adopted the point of view of many political scientists, that international relations are primarily relations among national states. Consequently, they have failed to stress inter-personal relations.

Furthermore, the leading texts uniformly fail to relate the major trends in American history to contemporary developments elsewhere in the world. For example, they fail to compare and contrast the Industrial Revolution in New England in the first half of the nineteenth century with the corresponding events in the old country a century earlier. They treat slavery, also, as a uniquely American institution. The reader gains no knowledge of the conditions in Africa, whence the slaves came. He is left in ignorance of the experience of other countries, Great Britain and Brazil, for example, in freeing their slaves. These omissions, which narrow the students' outlook on American history in the nineteenth century, lead to a false interpertation of twentieth-century events. American participation in the two great world wars and their aftermath is made to appear as a more radical departure from our historical traditions than it actually was.

Finally, the texts fail to provide the information about foreign countries which students must have if they are to fully grasp problems of American foreign policy. For example, postwar conflicts with the USSR usually receive brief attention in concluding chapters. But none of the leading texts in the field provides the information about the political and cultural heritage of the Russian people which is the necessary background for understanding the Cold War. The same weakness characterizes discussion of relations of the United States with Latin America and the Far East.

In general, the story of American foreign policy is told too exclusively from the American point of view. Its successes and failures are explained in terms of American interests, resources, and leadership, with inadequate attention to circumstances in the countries toward which our policies were directed, or upon which they impinged.

In reply to these strictures, it may be objected that the only purpose of an introductory American history course is to teach American history. To acquaint students with the major facts of the political and economic development of their own country, with some understanding of their interrelation and significance, is all that should be attempted in a single semester or even in a year. History textbooks are already overcrowded and, as each year provides new facts, the process becomes cumulative. The only solution to this problem is more rigid selection of material. The authors continually have to ask themselves such questions as this: Is it more important to make sure that students are thoroughly familiar with issues in the presidential campaign of 1828 or to see that they are acquainted with the conditions in foreign countries in the twentieth century which determined their response to our policies?

The answer is tied up with another question: What, after all, is the dominant purpose in teaching the elementary course in American history? Is it the preparation of a small group of young men and women to become specialists and to undertake research in the field, or should primary attention be given to the non-specialists who fill most of the seats in the classroom? Granted, they need to be acquainted with the major facts of national development. But to understand fully the significance of these internal facts, they need also to put American history in an international setting, to be able to understand the external forces that helped to mould it and the influences that the

United States has exerted abroad. Actually, a course thus motivated would not sacrifice the interests of the specialists. For them, an introductory course of a general character, stressing major facts and underscoring causal relations, could well be the best preparation for later advanced work of a more detailed nature.

GOVERNMENT–POLITICAL SCIENCE

In the introductory government course, or political science, enrollments everywhere are large: 700 at the University of Arizona; 1,500 at the University of Illinois; 800–900 each semester at Hunter College; and 3,000 at the University of Maryland. For this popularity, legislation, which in some states makes a course in American government a requirement for holders of teachers' certificates, is partly responsible. College statutes, moreover, often list the subject among the requirements for the bachelor's degree. Student preferences, also, play a part. Most students, when permitted an option among introductory courses in political science, take American government.

One might assume that because international relations is usually taught in departments of political science, the introductory course in the latter would show a strong emphasis on foreign affairs. However, the assumption would not be well-founded. Actually, the typical elementary course offered by departments of political science is devoted almost exclusively to description of the principal features of American government, and to the consideration of political processes in the United States. A 1950 survey[11] of introductory courses offered in 218 colleges and universities showed that 156 courses dealt primarily with domestic institutions, and that only 8 gave substantial attention to comparisons of American with foreign governments. A year later, a report of the American Political Science Association[12] reached a similar conclusion, viz., in a large majority of institutions of higher education the introductory courses concentrated on American government. The authors of the report, among them some of the leaders in the profession, strongly urged that the scope of the course be expanded. In most colleges and universities, their advice seems to have produced little effect. Some instructors have disregarded it, either out of inertia or because they disagreed. Others, while recognizing the need of giving their beginning students more knowledge of foreign political conditions and political problems, have been baffled by the problem of finding room for this material in an already overcrowded course. Mere addition of new facts, they feared, would make the entire treatment hopelessly superficial, but they were unwilling to face the task of radical revision.

In some states, legislation must bear responsibility for concentration on domestic affairs. Arizona, Illinois, Indiana, and other states require that holders of teachers' certificates for public school teaching must show they have been enrolled in a college course in American government. Frequently, local chapters of patriotic organizations are on the alert to see that such legislation is enforced.

Professor William M. Beaney of Princeton University, in a 1957 survey of 51 institutions,[13] found that the content of the introductory course had undergone little change since the publication in 1950 of the study by Thomas H. and Doris R. Reed. He reported:

The subject matter of the introductory political science course is prevalently U.S. national government, with some state and local materials added to most courses given at public institutions. Twenty-three of 26 public institutions devote all or a substantial part of their course to U.S. government. "Introduction to Politics" or some similar description characterizes all, or a substantial part, of the course in 6 institutions. One institution gives a semester of comparative government.

Private institutions are somewhat less partial to U.S. government, although 17 of 25 devote all or a substantial part of the course to this subject. Nine give theory and comparative, usually along with some U.S., and 2 have "Introduction to Politics" courses.

In the six-year interim which separated Professor Beaney's survey from that of the American Political Science Association, a significant change occurred in the goals at which teachers were aiming. In 1951, the Association's committee reported that citizenship training was generally regarded as the first objective of the introductory course. Intellectual stimulation of the students was listed second and cultivating a familiarity with political institutions, American and foreign, took third place. The emphasis on citizenship training placed the introductory course squarely in the category of general education and, unless "citizenship" was narrowly interpreted, one might expect that the course would give students some help in forming responsible opinions on matters of American foreign policy. But Professor Beaney, in 1957, found that the general education objective had disappeared. He wrote:

Most comments on "objectives" stressed the necessity of giving a student basic data and analytical skill *to prepare him for additional and more advanced courses in political science*. While it is argued that the typical introductory course is "good for the non-major," *one has the clear impression that the introductory course is not viewed generally as a course in citizenship training, or as a survey course for the non-major,* or as a means of arousing interest in politics in those who may enter the course without strong motivation. (Italics mine.) [14]

If these findings are correct, it seems that in representative colleges and universities the teaching of the introductory course in political science has not tended toward affording the common run of undergraduate more opportunities to learn about American foreign policy, international relations, and comparative government, but, rather, has moved in the reverse direction.

As presently taught, the course in the Elements of Political Science, according to a letter to the author from Professor R. W. Tucker of Johns Hopkins University, " . . . is almost always a course in American government with about two weeks spent on the conduct and control of foreign affairs and—if the instructor has any time left—on the substance of American foreign policy." The second semester, usually not required, ". . . consists of an introduction to government and society. Thus it is a general sketch of the basic problems of political science and will concentrate on the *internal problems of the state.*" (Italics mine.)

No generalization, even by the best informed observer, can accurately describe the content of an introductory course in government taught in hundreds of colleges by thousands of instructors. Many of them, according to training and experience, deviate more or less widely from the standard pattern of exclusive preoccupation with American government. The deviations are of three kinds: (1) greater emphasis on American foreign policy; (2) substitution of a conceptual approach for the prevalent emphasis on description and analysis; and (3) more attention to the operations of foreign governments and to the problems of international relations. All of these changes have taken place at Kenyon College:

In the present decade, the introductory course in Political Science has been converted gradually from a year course in American Government to a broad course covering modern political theory and ideologies, comparative government, international relations and the government of the United States. (Memorandum from Professor Raymond English.)

From one-half to two-thirds of all Kenyon students are exposed to the course.

The conceptual or philosophical approach, which is emphasized in the introductory courses at Brooklyn College, the University of Pittsburgh, Southwestern Louisiana Institute, Washington and Lee University, and other institutions, gives students a new and broader view of the principles and problems of government. They learn that the limitations on sovereignty, the use of force, the protection of the rights of the individual and minorities are universals—matters of vital concern in all forms of political organization—and not peculiar to the United States or any other national state. Each state, nevertheless, deals with them in its own fashion, according to its traditions and its economic and social environment. This philosophical approach to the study of government can be utilized to make students more perceptive regarding both their own political system and those of foreign countries.

Like all lower division courses in history and the social sciences, the introductory course in government is terminal for the common run of student—for all except the relatively small group who plan to specialize in history or in one of the social sciences. The great majority will never, in their four years of college, take another course in government. In most colleges, however, few of the instructing staff seem to feel the responsibility which this fact lays upon them.

Where the introductory course occupies a full year, one semester is often devoted to comparative government. At Harvard, the general course in government begins with a brief study of the governments of the principal foreign powers. This is followed in the second semester by political theory. Yale

College's big course, Elements of Government and Politics, devotes one semester to comparative governments. At Trinity College (Connecticut), the first term of the course called Modern Government deals with the structure and problems of European governments. The Department of Political Science at Westmnister College (Pennsylvania) has replaced a course in state and local government with a course in comparative government.

Teachers who stress comparative government in the elementary political science course are not aiming exclusively, or even primarily, at imparting information about foreign countries, or increasing their students' understanding of foreign institutions. They believe that the comparison and contrast of American government with foreign governments can give the American college student a deeper understanding of political institutions and procedures in his own country. However, the realization of this goal is obstructed when, in the study of foreign governments, predominant attention is given to description of constitutional and administrative structures, with corresponding neglect of the factors, historical and environmental, which have influenced them.

An elective course in comparative government is often offered separately, rather than as a part of the introductory course. Examination of the most recent catalogs of our sample of 36 colleges and universities (see Chapter 2) shows that 33 of them offered courses in comparative government. In about half of the courses, lower division students were admitted. The evidence from our sample of 1,563 students' records from these institutions indicates that the course was not popular with the typical undergraduate. Altogether, only 122 students, 7.8 percent of the total, were found to have taken it.

More than 60 percent of them had majors in history or the social sciences.

TEXTBOOKS IN GOVERNMENT. Examination of the leading textbooks used in the introductory course in government bears out the comments already made on its ethnocentric character; all are sharply focused on government in the United States. Their occasional allusions to the problems of government in foreign countries are brief and sketchy. The authors mention the indebtedness of American jurisprudence to English common law, and devote a few pages to comparisons of the British and American constitutional systems. All contain a chapter or two on American foreign policy which consider processes of policy-making and administration. Sections on political behavior occasionally make comparisons with foreign countries, but scattered through hundreds of pages of text, they can hardly add in any significant manner to students' information about political institutions in foreign countries.

ECONOMICS

The introductory course in economics is regularly viewed with disfavor by lower division students. They regard it as "the scourge of the campus." "Ec 1" at Harvard is described, in a student publication, as " . . . . a monster that the Department doesn't quite know what to do with. The course has great potential, little of which has been realized."[15] Faculty members are inclined to agree. Professor T. L. Carlson of Western Michigan University has referred to the basic principles course as " . . . an overloaded and disorderly grab-bag of miscellaneous data and unrelated items. . . . "[16] Another well-known teacher described principles of economics as " . . . deadly, impractical, and probably the worst taught course in American colleges and universities."[17] These, of course, are extreme statements; they apply, as the American Economic Association's committee remarked, to colleges where teaching schedules are heavy and admission standards low. Where conditions are more favorable, instruction is more effective and student interest is higher; but even in colleges where the best standards prevail, teachers and students express dissatisfaction.

Elementary economics, nevertheless, constitutes one of the principal traffic points in the lower division curriculum. Yearly enrollments run from 100 to 200 at independent liberal arts colleges of moderate size, to 500 at Yale, 750 at the Massachusetts Institute of Technology, 1,000 at the University of Pittsburgh, and 1,200 at Harvard and the University of California (Berkeley campus).

Distribution requirements partly explain the paradox. Economics regularly may be offered in partial fulfillment of the social science or general education requirement. Schools of engineering, and other professional schools, often require all their students to take the course. The requirement is practically universal in schools of business administration. Consequently, at some state universities the school of business furnishes the bulk of the students in the elementary course in economics. For example, in 1959–60, business school students at the University of Indiana made up 85 percent of the enrollment (650 all told) in the introductory course. Where this situation exists, the emphasis in the course is apt to be on professional training rather than on general education.

Elementary economics contributes little, probably less than any other introductory course in the social sciences, to the students' stock of information about conditions and institutions in foreign countries. It adds little to their understanding of the economic aspects of American foreign policy or of international relations in general. In fact, these matters now prob-ably receive less attention in the introductory course than was accorded them half a century ago. This results from continual addition of new material primarily concerned with the domes-tic economy, such as national income accounting and the eco-nomics of the individual firm. At present, across the country, in little colleges and big universities, elementary economics deals principally with economic theories and with *domestic* econom-ic policies—the farm problem, problems of organized labor, and the relation of government to business. Its emphasis is on the description and the operation of the American economic system.

Foreign affairs, in the usual two-semester, six-hour course, receive consideration at three points: in discussions of econom-ic growth and development in underdeveloped countries; in chapters on comparative economic systems which contrast the operation of the Soviet and the American economies; and in sections on international trade and finance. Taken altogether, these matters rarely occupy more than 10 or 15 percent of the total number of class periods.[18] As often happens, an instructor may omit one or more of these topics when he is pressed for time.

REVISION AND REFORM. Teachers who have given serious thought to the improvement of courses in elements of econom-ics, or economic principles, recognize that, for the bulk of the students who are enrolled, the course is terminal; it repre-sents their only exposure to economics in their four years of college. Consequently, its purpose, they believe, should be to provide general education in the subject and not to prepare specialists in economics or in business administration. To carry out this principle, they propose to cut down the number of topics treated. They would either eliminate entirely certain specialized subjects, such as corporate finance, the security markets, social insurance, and the regulation of public utilities, or deal with them in shorter compass and in a less technical fashion. From the treatment of theories of value and market prices, they would remove much of the mathematical apparatus which now bewilders the beginning student. These and other changes would make it possible to concentrate attention on a relatively few general subjects of prime importance—the nature of the economic problem, the landmarks of economic theory, the general functions of economic systems, and the characteristic features of the American economy.

An active program of reform, based on these and similar ideas, has been set in motion by the Joint Council on Economic Education (J.C.E.E.), an organization financed by grants from the Ford Foundation, the Committee on Economic Development, and other organizations. The Council focuses its attention on improving the education in economics of prospective and in-service secondary school teachers of social studies.[19] To give them a better understanding of what economics is all about, it has had prepared outlines and text materials which, with some modification, might be effectively used by college freshmen. But the J.C.E.E. project, and some others, for converting elementary economics from a specialized to a general course, reveal one significant weakness: they deal with the American economy as an isolated phenomenon. Economic aspects of international relations, the place of the United States in the world economy, and the country's foreign economic policy are subjects to which the revisionists have, as yet, paid scant attention. In defense of this neglect, some cite the plethora of subjects that have to be "covered," even after nonessentials have been eliminated. Their business, they say, is to teach economics, not foreign affairs. A few, however, recognize that international trade and economic development really are not extraneous matters; they belong in the corpus of the discipline and can contribute to the orderly exposition of economic principles.

This belief inspires the course Economics I, Economic Institutions in the Pattern of Economic Growth, at Brooklyn College, newly revised by a committee of the Department of Economics. Built around the concept of economic development, the course contrasts the rapid economic growth of Western Europe, the United States, and Canada in the past 150 years, and in Russia in the last generation, with the continued backwardness of much of the rest of the world. Thus, at the very beginning of the course at Brooklyn, the students become involved in discussions of political and cultural factors in economic development, including American policies of foreign aid. These matters are not, as in most introductory courses, treated as peripheral, to be considered or disregarded according to the convenience of the instructor. Instead, they are shown to be vitally connected with the health and growth of the domestic economy and with domestic policy.

ANTHROPOLOGY AND SOCIOLOGY

Recent developments in the foreign policies of the United States, and of other countries, have tended to arouse the interest of sociologists and anthropologists in international relations. The "revolution of rising expectations" has brought primitive peoples—roughly one-third of the world's population—from the wings of the international stage to the footlights. Hence, the teaching of cultural and physical anthropology has taken on new significance. What are the capabilities of the native inhabitants of either Burma or Nigeria for economic development and for self-government? Are they innately inferior to the white race, or is their backwardness a result of an unfavorable physical and cultural environment? These are no longer questions of academic interest; legislators and their constituents are asking them and giving answers, of some sort, every day.

In anthropology, instructors in the introductory course focus their attention on the physical and psychological characteristics of primitive men. Neither the instructors nor their students are directly concerned with either foreign policy or international relations. Nevertheless, a significant by-product of the course may be a better understanding of our foreign aid policies and the factors that condition the struggle between the United States and the USSR for the allegiance of the underdeveloped and uncommitted countries.

For the non-specialist, the introductory course in anthropology affords one of his few opportunities to make the acquaintance of alien, i.e., non-Western, cultures. Besides providing new information, courses in anthropology may affect students' attitudes toward foreigners. Professor Louise M. Rosenblatt has written:

They [the anthropologists] have reinforced our awareness of the amazing diversity of social patterns that men have created—strikingly different modes of behavior, types of personal relationships, ideas of good and evil, religious beliefs, social organizations, economic and political mechanisms, and forms of art. But the anthropologists find these differences evidence only of the extreme plasticity of the human creature. They have made us understand that men have fashioned these divergent patterns of living out of the raw materials of their common humanity, out of the common drives which all human beings share.[20]

New developments in the strategy and tactics of foreign policy have opened new fields of interest for the sociologists. The widening scope of cultural activities which are conducted across national boundaries has drawn attention to inter-personal and inter-group activities in the field of foreign affairs. Such activities, it is true, are often guided and ultimately may be controlled by national states; nevertheless, they represent a rather novel aspect of international relations—one which is of particular interest to the behavioral scientists. Falling within their field, also, are official and semi-official propaganda, particularly radio broadcasting, which aims to influence the policies of hostile or friendly states, not directly, but through appeals to public opinion.

The basic course in sociology, in many colleges occupying a whole year, in others a semester or a quarter, represents one of the major traffic points in undergraduate education. Unlike corresponding courses in American history and government, it is not a requirement for holders of teachers' certificates in public schools. Nevertheless, enrollments are uniformly large, in some institutions exceeding those in the introductory courses in economics and government. Some freshmen and sophomores may choose sociology as the easiest course to fulfill a distribution requirement. Many are drawn into the course by intellectual curiosity, but only a few intend to specialize in sociology; for most students the introductory course is terminal.

No easy generalization is possible regarding the contribution which introductory sociology makes to students' knowledge about foreign countries. In this respect, variations, depending on the intellectual climate of institutions and on the interests and capacities of teachers, appear to be even wider than in political science or economics. In some colleges, members of the teaching staff who have had the advantage of living for a number of years abroad inevitably will make frequent references to social stratification, family systems, etc., in foreign countries. At Hunter College, eight of the 20 members of the instructional staff in introductory sociology have had foreign experience; at the University of Kansas, five out of 10 have done field work abroad or have taught in foreign universities; at the University of California in Los Angeles, all but five of the 31 persons teaching the introductory course have had experience abroad.

At Louisiana State University, the main goal of the introductory course is the comparative study of societies. At Carleton College, teaching about social institutions in foreign countries, particularly Russia and China, is regarded as one of the purposes of the introductory course. At Emory University, about one-third of the course deals directly with social institutions and conditions abroad. Teachers, in these and other colleges, who lay stress on comparative studies do not have in mind primarily spreading information about foreign countries. Comparisons, in their opinion, are essential to the orderly development of their subject and indispensable for understanding the basic institutions of American society. For example, the purpose of the course Human Society and Culture, taught by Professor June Collins at Michigan State (Oakland), as stated in the syllabus, is "to find out what is general or universal in human society and . . . through contrasts, to gain insight into our own society." A similarly broad approach characterizes the introductory courses at Brooklyn College, Rollins, the University of California at Berkeley, and the University of Pittsburgh.

The introductory course at Westminster College (Pennsylvania), according to Professor C. P. Edwards, is taught "as a universal discipline, not simply limited to the United States models and systems." The conceptual approach to sociology, illustrated in this statement, usually involves the discussion of foreign as well as American institutions. Teachers who adopt this approach stress certain fundamental principles which are manifested in varying ways in human societies all over the world. Others reject it, claiming that the common run of student, even with the assistance of comparative data, finds abstract thinking too difficult. Nevertheless, instructors, both at the University of Florida, which has a liberal admissions policy, and at the University of California, which is highly selective, use the conceptual approach and are satisfied with the results.

Interviews and correspondence with teachers of sociology indicate that emphasis on concepts and comparisons of foreign and domestic institutions is not uniformly found in introductory courses in sociology. Instead, in a great many, perhaps in the majority, reading materials and class discussions center on American social institutions, American social conditions, and American social problems. Moreover, "American sociology" is not a regional phenomenon; it is taught in Pennsylvania, Maine, Indiana, and California, as well as in Georgia and South Carolina.

TEXTBOOKS IN SOCIOLOGY. Examination of leading textbooks[21] lends support to the view that introductory sociology, as taught in many colleges and universities, perhaps in the majority, falls short of making substantial contributions to students' knowledge and understanding of foreign countries.

In the preface to his *Sociology*, Arnold Green states that he has kept two questions constantly in mind: "Where is American society now?" and "Where is it likely to go?" The primary purpose of an elementary textbook, he believes, " . . . is to aid the student in acquiring an understanding of his own society." Nevertheless, he asserts that in the book "the unity, integration, and universality of social relationships *in all times and places* receive due consideration." (Italics mine.) He has more thoroughly performed the first part of his twofold task than the second. After some general and theoretical considerations, in Part I, there follows a series of chapters devoted exclusively to the American scene. The titles are: "Class and Mobility in America," "The American Economic Order," "The American Political Order," etc. The index contains two references to Russia, but no mention of India or China. Population statistics, birth and death rates, age distribution, etc., constitute the largest single block of information on foreign countries in this book.

Ogburn and Nimkoff's *Sociology* has an excellent chapter on the distribution of population, well illustrated by maps showing the influence of climate and topography. It describes the postwar population shifts of the USSR and Western Europe. In the Introduction, the authors recognize their obligation not only to sociology majors but to all students as well. They assert that a beginning text in sociology should have two purposes: (1) to enable students to live intelligently in the social world around them and (2) to fit them to become leaders of opinion and action in their communities. But their concepts of "the social world," and of the "communities" in which the students would live after graduation, seem to have been narrow. Their discussions of social stratification, of the organization of family life, and of culture and personality, contain illustrations which are drawn predominantly from the American scene. For the most part, references to similar aspects of social life abroad are to the life of primitive peoples rather than to contemporary modern societies. Regarding the latter, the student is informed that the suicide rate is higher in Protestant than in Catholic countries; that Sweden has a lower divorce rate than the United States and that it is culturally less homogeneous than Ceylon; that the British are a disciplined people, that they enjoy a greater degree of freedom of speech than is permitted in the United States, and that they have not been as much affected as the Americans by anti-Communist hysteria.

Broom and Selznick, from the point of view of this study, do a better job. In a series of brief adaptations of scholarly articles, they give their readers thumbnail sketches of special aspects of foreign cultures, modern as well as primitive. The topics include Negro-Pygmy relations in Africa, the effects of the intrusion of new political ideas on family and community life in a small rural village in Japan, social stratification in Soviet Russia, comparisons of population statistics for India and the United States, fertility of marriages in Ceylon, and racial policies in South Africa. These selections are useful in illustrating sociological principles; they may stimulate students' curiosity about foreign countries, but they provide only scattered bits of information. Their principal contribution appears to lie in the realm of attitudes rather than in that of facts. By inducing an objective view of social customs and institutions, the authors may help students to approach problems of international relations in a detached fashion, and to avoid, in forming their judgments, the distorting effects of racial or religious bias.

GEOGRAPHY

College students know little geography. This opinion is often expressed by teachers in departments of history and international relations. Yet geography, if properly taught, can make a fundamental contribution to students' knowledge and understanding of foreign countries. In fact, it is hard to see how a young man or woman who can't locate the NATO countries or the Soviet satellites on the map of Europe, or who thinks that the Suez Canal separates North from South America, can intelligently deal with the problems of American foreign policy. Economic geography, obviously, is essential to the understanding of the policies of international trade and economic aid.

Geography, nevertheless, has generally been a neglected study in secondary schools, and in colleges and universities as well. A great majority of college freshmen have had no training in geography in high school. A recent Michigan survey revealed that only 6 percent of the high school students in that state had been exposed to formal courses in geography; and that usually a college freshman's last contact with that subject occurred in the sixth grade. High school geography, on the whole, is badly taught. Few schools can afford a well-trained specialist; hence, the subject is often taught in rotation, for a term or two, by poorly prepared men and women whose major interests are in other fields. Since questions on geography do not appear in college entrance examinations, the brighter pupils, who are planning to go to college, avoid the subject. Geography classes in many schools have become the refuge of the dullards.

In college, freshmen and sophomores, affected perhaps by the bad reputation which geography has acquired in high school, are less likely to choose elementary geography than some other social science to fulfill their distribution requirements. To this rule, there are exceptions. In some institutions, introductory courses in geography have large enrollments, but for reasons which appear to have little relevance to the educational value of the subject. At Hunter College, majors in the social science group, which comprise about one-fourth of all students, have to choose either geography or statistics to fulfill a distribution requirement. Most of them find geography more attractive. As a result, between one-half and two-thirds of all Hunter College students are enrolled, at some time or other in their four years, in elementary geography. At the University of Kansas, where geography is classified as a natural science, about 400 students annually choose geography as an alternative to subjects such as mathematics, physics, and chemistry which have a tougher reputation. Despite these exceptional enrollments, it is generally true that relatively few students are exposed to a formal course in geography during their college careers. Benjamin Fine, in his 1950 survey of 250 colleges and universities, reported: "Fewer than 5 percent of the college students in this country are taking even one geography course this academic year . . . the nation's colleges and universities virtually ignore the teaching of geography."[22]

College geography has suffered the neglect of an ill-favored stepchild. No one seems to know where the subject belongs. In some institutions, it finds shelter among the social sciences; in others, it has been adopted, but not well nurtured, by the geologists. The most interesting features of the discipline, which might have attracted the common run of undergraduate as well as advanced students, have been absorbed by the social sciences. Historians, economists, political scientists, anthropologists, all teach geography. Thus, the subject has become the battleground of jurisdictional disputes which eventually have left the authentic geographers with exclusive rights only in spatial orientation, the bare bones of their subject.

In privately-supported colleges and universities, geography receives scant attention. Harvard, in 1956–57, discontinued practically all of its course offerings. The 1958–59 catalog lists only two courses: The Historical Geography of England and a Seminar in Historical Geography, primarily for graduates. At Princeton, the Department of Geology lists a single course, Physical Geography. The 1960 *Directory of College Geography of the United States*[23] reported that 457 schools, 27 percent of the 1,668 institutions from which reports were received, had no formal work in geography. The majority of these were private institutions. It is true that in some privately-supported colleges and universities, for example, at Yale and Columbia, highly qualified scholars are providing excellent instruction for small groups of graduate students and advanced under-graduates, but they fail to attract any substantial number of lower division students into the introductory courses.

Recently, geography seems to be gaining a stronger position as a general education subject. Registration in introductory courses appears to be increasing, both absolutely and in rela-tion to all geography enrollments. The 1960 *Directory* showed that, of the 314,633 students enrolled in college courses in geography, 127,650—41 percent of the total—were in intro-ductory courses. Comparison of 1960 data with the 1952 fig-ures shows a 26 percent increase in all courses, but a 46 percent gain in those designed for beginners in the subject. About one-half of the total increase in geography enrollments in the eight years took place in introductory courses. At the same time, the courses have undergone changes which make them a more rewarding educational experience. Physical and politi-cal geography are giving way to regional or world geography.

The best of the new courses in world geography do not attempt to "cover" the whole world by describing, even briefly, all its regions. Instead, they aim to teach students certain elementary ways of looking at a limited number of regions in order that they may perceive and understand significant differences. Courses of this sort train students to deal with concepts and principles instead of memorizing a multitude of geographical facts. The lack of good textbooks hampers the effective teaching of world geography on the college level. More significant, probably, is the shortage of geographers who are interested in developing their subject as general education and who have the training necessary to do so effectively.

4. Non-Western Civilizations

American colleges and universities only recently have become aware of the need to give undergraduates more opportunities to learn about countries loosely described as "non-Western." This term, which usually comprises Russia and Eastern Europe, the Far East and Africa, and sometimes Latin America as well, I use reluctantly. Aside from the fact that undergraduates know little about them—even less than about Western Europe—the countries in the non-Western group have no unifying characteristic, either geographic, economic, political, or cultural. To describe Latin America as "non-Western" does violence to geography. Ecuador has no cultural links with Iran. The political institutions and aspirations of Red China have little in common with those of Argentina. Economically, many of the so-called non-Western countries could be described as "underdeveloped," but this term would not appy to Japan, and only by much stretching could it cover both the USSR and Ethiopia. Nevertheless, because "non-Western" is current, and because no alternate short, accurate expression is available, it will be used in the following pages.

In 1947, the President's Commission on Higher Education said:

In the past the liberal arts college has stressed the history, arts, and institutions of Western culture, without giving much time or attention to the kinds of civilization that exist in other parts of the globe. In the new world it is not enough to know and understand our own heritage. Modern man needs to sense the sweep of world history in order to see his own civilization in the context of other cultures.[1]

Since this was written, political events have proved the wisdom of the Committee's advice. With the breakdown of the old colonial system, during and after World War II, many new states were set up in Asia and Africa. Their efforts to establish themselves in the international arena and to provide a better life for their people have introduced new problems for the statesmen of the United States and other Western countries. Immediately after the Second World War, Western Europe was the focus of United States foreign policy. After 1950, the conflict in Korea shifted the center of attention to the Far East. The dramatic Suez affair and the long-drawn-out struggle of France to subdue nationalist Moslems in Algeria made Americans aware of the conflicts in the Middle East. Now the sudden emergence, in Africa, south of the Sahara, of many new national states and their acceptance into the United Nations, has injected a new non-Western element into that body, with results on American foreign policy that are still unpredictable.

This new situation in international affairs has presented a new challenge to higher education in the United States. College graduates of the 1960s need a much wider acquaintance with the world than did their parents. To the new challenge, the response of the colleges has been both tardy and inadequate. In the social sciences, introductory courses in politics and economics, as far as they deal at all with foreign countries, still refer only to those in Western Europe. Sociologists, because of their interest in primitive peoples, show more concern for the non-Western world. But courses in international relations still give attention principally to the affairs of the members of the North Atlantic Treaty Organization, and courses in the humanities are concerned primarily with Western cultural traditions. In church-related colleges active in foreign missionary work, Oriental studies have long figured in the undergraduate curriculum. Elsewhere, they have been pursued mostly by graduate students.

Courses and Enrollments

A 1955 survey, conducted for the Conference on Asian Affairs, Inc., found that only 60 percent of American institutions of higher learning offered undergraduates courses relating wholly or in significant part to Asia.[2] The survey also found that opportunities for the study of Asia were concentrated in a limited number of institutions (two-thirds of the courses were offered in 275 of the 1,367 institutions studied) and that they reached relatively few students. From these and other data in the Conference's report, Mortimer Graves, Director of the American Council of Learned Societies, concluded that "by far the largest proportion of Americans who graduate from institutions of higher learning do so without ever meeting a civilization differently patterned from their own."[3] Since 1955, many new courses have been established dealing with Asia, Africa, and other non-European areas; but the advance has occurred principally in the larger institutions. Thus, " . . . the gap is widening between the institutions that are doing the least and those that are doing the most to make their students intellectually aware of the non-Western world."[4]

Examination of the catalogs of the 36 representative colleges and universities listed in Chapter 2 shows that all offered at least one course dealing with Asia, Africa, or Russia and Eastern Europe. The total number of courses offered was 552, but the distribution was uneven. A group of 13 institutions listed 400 courses, 72 percent of the total.

An area breakdown gives the following results: Asia, 31 institutions offered one or more courses with a total of 237 courses available; Africa, 22 institutions offered one or more courses with a total of 34 courses available; Latin America, 30 institutions offered one or more courses with a total of 152 courses available; and Russia and Eastern Europe, 35 institutions offered one or more courses with a total of 129 courses available.

Non-specializing students in these institutions showed little interest in non-Western courses. Our analysis of the academic records of 1,645 students shows that only 292—slightly more than one in six—had taken at least one course dealing with the geography, history, the economic or political situation of a non-Western country during their four years in college.

An area breakdown shows that students were enrolled in one or more of the courses as follows: Asia, 82; Africa, 10; Latin America, 66; and Russia and Eastern Europe, 62.

Most of the non-Western courses offered to undergraduates are concerned with Asia, the Far East, or Latin America. But since the end of World War II, offerings in the history and economic organization of the USSR have rapidly increased; also, courses in the Russian language and literature. At present, in every state in the union, instruction in the Russian language is available to college students. In Indiana, interest in non-Western areas is centered on Russian history. A 1957–58 survey of 34 institutions of higher education in that state showed that

13 offered courses in Russian history, either annually or in alternate years. In a single year, however, they enrolled only 340 (0.5 percent) of Indiana's 65,000 undergraduate students.[5]

Courses giving undergraduates opportunity to learn about Africa are hard to find. The Cultural Planning and Coordination Staff of the Department of State, in 1959, listed 31 institutions "currently offering area training, research or course work on Africa . . . " but only 13 offered courses to which undergraduates were admitted.

In many colleges and universities, large and small, teachers and administrators feel that they ought to do more in the field of non-Western studies, but they are uncertain what they should do. "The most urgent problem," according to Professor Robert Byrnes of Indiana University, "is to determine how to expose all, or practically all, undergraduates to the non-Western world in some form."[6] But in what form? Do area courses provide the answer, or survey courses, or perhaps a combination of both?

Area Courses

Students who wish to specialize in a non-Western civilization may enroll either in a course offered by a single department (e.g., history of Russia), or in an interdisciplinary or "area" course. The latter may be taught either by a team of members of various departments—usually history, government, economics, sociology, anthropology—or by a single professor bold enough to invade the territories of other departments. When first introduced, after World War II, area courses provided intensive training for graduate students; later, these courses trickled down to the undergraduate level, but still were designed principally for specialists.

Area courses usually have a practical slant. They emphasize

current situations, and, hence, are popular with upperclassmen preparing for jobs in industry, government, or academic institutions. But there are noteworthy exceptions. In two area courses at Brooklyn College, The Far East and The Caribbean Area and Latin America, the vocational goal is explicitly rejected. Instead, the aim is to train non-specialists in a new way of thinking about foreign countries and their peoples. At the University of Oregon, many area studies "are designed to attract students who elect them for general education purposes." The courses in the University of Chicago's interdisciplinary Asian program serve two purposes: as components of "a common core of liberal education" and as a background for specialized studies.

General Courses in Non-Western Civilizations

General courses in Asian or other non-Western civilizations are designed to form part of a liberal education. The overriding purpose is to stimulate the student's intellectual curiosity, to break through the "barriers of cultural ignorance," and to round out his knowledge of the world. Columbia's Oriental Studies Program introduces non-specialists—pre-medical, pre-engineering, and pre-law students—not just social science majors, to the most general features of the major Oriental civilizations. Of this program, Professor de Bary has written:

There are many persons today who explain the need for Asian studies in terms of the rising importance of Asian peoples in the world today, of their crucial role in the East-West struggle, and of the necessity for Asian-American understanding as the basis of an effective foreign policy. There is no question but that such considerations are vital in the political, diplomatic, and military arena today, but there is a very real question whether they have anything to do with liberal education. The peoples and civilizations of Asia are important to undergraduate education, not because they represent factors in the cold war, as means to some immediate practical end, but because their experience in living together, what they have learned about life, and what they have come to understand about the universe we all live in is now part of the common human heritage. Nor are these peoples to be studied like problem children needing our help. They are to be studied, rather, as peoples who can teach us much about ourselves, whose past can give us a new perspective on our own, and whose way of looking at things can challenge us to a re-examination of our own.[7]

General courses in non-Western civilizations are usually designed for lower division students. Columbia's two-year sequence in Oriental civilizations and Harvard's Far Eastern civilization do not admit freshmen. But the University of Minnesota's course, History of Asia, introduced in 1959, has students from all classes, two-thirds of them in the lower division. At the University of Arizona, Introduction to Far Eastern Civilizations, given in the Department of Anthropology as well as in the Department of History, is open to both lower and upper division students (enrollment, first semester 1959–60, was 106 students). In 1958, the University of Michigan introduced a course on Asian civilizations which is open *only to freshmen and sophomores*.

PROBLEMS OF THE GENERAL COURSE

The introduction of a new course on non-Western civilizations, of the general education type, raises two problems: (1) How to find a place for it in already crowded curricula; and (2) How to make sure that it enrolls a substantial number of the common run of students, and is not populated exclusively by specialists. In a few of the larger and richer institutions it may prove feasible to maintain two parallel general education courses, in Oriental civilization and in Western civilization, as at Columbia University. But the resources of most institutions, in money and in men, would not permit such an undertaking. Besides, there is the question of enrollments. Few colleges would consider making the new non-Western course a requirement for graduation, especially if Western Civilization is already a required subject. But when a non-Western course is offered *as an elective*, students' response is only moderate. Chicago's series of four courses on Asia have a combined enrollment of 150 undergraduates each year. Columbia's Oriental Civilizations has 150; Harvard's History of Far Eastern Civilization enrolls 200.

The new course will be successful in broadening the cultural horizon of the average student only if it has large enrollments; ideally, at least half of the freshmen and sophomores should participate. Progress toward general participation can be achieved by including the course among the distribution requirements in the social sciences, or in the humanities. Student counsellors should make clear to the students who rely on them for guidance, the advantages of acquaintance with a non-Western civilization.

All survey courses run the danger of superficiality. Critics question ". . . the wisdom of requiring so many to devote so little time to so much."[8] Superficiality may be avoided by skillful application of the block and gap method. Of its use in the introductory course on Asia at the University of Michigan, Professor Robert I. Crane has written:

. . . By this means we emphasize a certain block of material on one aspect of a major Asian cultural tradition but do not necessarily treat that same aspect when dealing with the other major cultural traditions of Asia. By judicious choice of the topics dealt with in *each* of the major cultures, we attempt to provide an adequate coverage of all three traditions [viz., the Islamic, the Indic and the Sinitic] without sacrificing depth of analysis. We do not try to cover every aspect of each culture in Asia, nor do we try to cover all aspects of the three major cultures. We do try, wherever possible, to illuminate *an* important facet of life or culture in Asia by reference in some depth to its manifestation in *one* of the major cultures.[9]

Some educators would reject the general course, even if ideally organized. They point out the impossibility of making a clean-cut separation of the non-Western civilizations from the Western; in the culture of a typically Western country, such as the United States or France, there are many elements of Oriental origin. In some countries, as in the USSR, the inheritance of both Western and Eastern cultures makes classification in either of the two groups hard to defend. Moreover, as Professor Weiner has observed, it may be bad education to try to put East and West in separate categories. ". . . A view of the world divided into a West and a non-West may create greater stereotypes than some of those we are trying to undo."[10]

From a different point of view, others object to a course devoted exclusively to Asian or Oriental civilizations. Asia, to them, represents not a field of study but a whole world of culture; hence, Asian material should not be presented in chunks but should be integrated into courses already established in the various disciplines. Thus, concern about Asia, Africa, and other non-Western countries would lose something of its exotic quality and become part of the undergraduates' normal academic experience.[11]

"Infiltration" rather than integration is the word used to describe the method adopted in the Asian Studies Program at Denison University. The initial point of attack is the faculty. The program is designed ". . . to stimulate further interest in Asian affairs within the faculty," thereby promoting a greater diffusion of Asian materials in the curriculum. "Specifically, the aim is not a proliferation of new courses on Asia or a new major in Asian studies but rather the introduction of Asian material for illustrative and comparative purposes into existing courses. In this way it is hoped the curriculum may be reoriented somewhat from its present almost exclusively Western base. . . ."[12] In this vein, President Phillips of Bates College has suggested that present courses in many fields, particularly the introductory courses, should be reworked so as to include Eastern culture. ". . . Thus an introductory sociology course may make reference to conditions in Rangoon as well as in Chicago; the mathematics course may stress our debt to the Asians as well as to the Germans; the basic biology course may emphasize research in Russia as well as that in the United States."[13]

The Combination of Area Courses with General Courses

Infiltration of introductory courses in various disciplines with non-Western material will add to the undergraduate's stock of information about many far-away countries, but may leave him in a state of hazy uncertainty about any one of them. Even though he doesn't aim to be an expert in any nation or region, still he would find it useful, as part of his general education, to dig into the history and culture of some corner of an alien civilization. Marshall Hodgson has written that for many students the study of *one* major culture, in its heritage and in its present problems, can give us more insight into our modern world than a superficial review of all non-Western peoples:

Concentration for a year on a single civilization offers, in addition, the unique advantage of allowing the student gradually, and on the basis of a rich variety of contrasting cultural strains within the whole, to form an image of a total developing civilization diverse and yet united over time and space. This is perhaps scarcely possible in the case of his own Western civilization, mediated to him from so many courses and other sources and within which he must take his own position. But if it can be achieved in the case of another major culture, he may come closer to such an insight in the case of his own.[14]

Ward Morehouse has warned against the tendency to put area studies ". . . somewhere on the periphery of the main stream of academic life of the college community." The great task of the coming decade, he foresees, will be ". . . to enlarge the intellectual and cultural horizons of all college students and we are not going to do this if we simply insert a course here or there in an obscure corner of the curriculum which attracts a few students."[15] In order to relate area studies more closely to the undergraduate curriculum, a number of institutions have worked out plans, or are making plans, whereby every undergraduate's program will include both a general survey course and a specialized course dealing with a non-Western area. Indiana University is considering a course in non-Western civilization which would be required for all students in the College of Arts and Sciences. This is a first step in an Asian Studies Program which proposes eventually to provide every undergraduate with knowledge of non-Western societies. Western College for Women supplements its four-year cycle of area courses with a required course in The Development of World Civilizations. This is an interdisciplinary effort in which 30 faculty members collaborate. Colgate requires students to choose one area course from a list of seven, four of which deal with non-Western areas. All seniors must enroll, also, in a survey course—America Confronts the World Community. All students at the New York State College of Education at New Paltz must take a course in Western civilization and, in addition, a course in Asian civilization and a course on Africa and the Near East.

At the University of Minnesota, the committee in charge of

interdisciplinary programs has suggested that for each area, or sub-area, there should be an introductory survey course at the lower division level. Such a course would provide general education for students who go no further in the subject. The Committee had another objective in mind—the potential specialists. It hoped that the new courses might serve as "feeders" for major programs.

The University of South Florida, a branch of the state's system of higher education, opened at Tampa in October, 1960, will offer a number of area courses as undergraduate electives. In this case, specialization will precede generalization. The student, either in his freshman or sophomore year, will choose a course in some non-Western culture. In his senior year, he may take a course which compares characteristic features of several cultures.

To promote a general understanding of the world community is one of the aims which has guided curriculum development at the new Michigan State University (Oakland) opened in October, 1960. Understanding of the non-Western world was considered "crucial for the leadership of the next generation." As one means of accomplishing this objective, the curriculum combines area courses with a basic course in the history and development of Western civilization. According to present plans, this course, required for all freshmen, will be followed in the junior year by a group of full-year courses in several non-Western culture areas, from which each student will be required to choose one.

At San Francisco State College, the area studies approach is employed, experimentally, in teaching a general education course in international relations. In 1959–60, four sections of the required one-semester course concentrated on China. Each section was taught by a single instructor with Far Eastern training and experience. Professor Urban Whitaker,[16] who has had principal responsibility for introducing the area approach, notes among its advantages the stimulation of a high degree of motivation among both students and instructors. The instructors find it more rewarding to use their knowledge of a single area as a vehicle for instruction in international relations than to attempt to teach international relations either in the abstract or with reference to 80 or more individual national states. Students take more interest in studying Chinese nationalism than nationalism as a global phenomenon. Also, by concentrating on the political, economic, and cultural characteristics of a single national state, they are helped to develop a sense of empathy, to project themselves into the daily lives, and the thoughts and emotional experiences of its inhabitants, and perhaps of other areas by a process of transfer. A further advantage claimed for the area approach to international relations is that it provides the student, and the instructor, with a natural or logical way of interrelating subject matter drawn from many disciplines.

The sponsors of the new method recognize certain dangers in its use. Single areas may fail to offer good illustrations of every important type of international activity. There is also the danger that students may become so absorbed in learning new facts about a strange country or region that they give only secondary attention to the principal aim of the course, learning about international relations. To determine whether or not, on balance, the new approach provides a more effective method of teaching than the old, the staff of the course have been running a series of achievement tests by which the progress in learning of students in the experimental sections can be compared with the gains in sections taught by traditional methods.

Teachers and Teaching Materials

Lack of adequately prepared teachers and well-planned, well-written texts hamper the introduction of all types of courses in non-Western civilizations. Their wide scope and the diversity of cultures which, in some fashion or other, they must cover makes the construction of a good text particularly difficult. In institutions where a highly selective admissions policy has produced a student body that is unusually alert and well-prepared, the ponderous, all-inclusive text is being replaced either by collections of source materials or by the increasingly numerous, well-written "paperbacks." Elsewhere, the textbook will continue to hold its position for some time. It is an essential aid to instructors who, without adequate preparation, are called upon to teach Asian, African, or some other non-Western civilization.

THE STAFFING PROBLEM

In staffing non-Western courses, both the general education type and area courses, heads of departments encounter a double difficulty. Teachers who have special knowledge of Asia or the Far East, Latin America, Russia, and particularly of Africa are in short supply. Moreover, those who have acquired such knowledge through years of study, travel, and, perhaps, extended residence abroad are apt to be more interested in research, or in teaching small groups of graduate students and advanced undergraduates, than in giving a general course. They may recognize that their own training in graduate school has left them poorly prepared for such a task. Ambitious young men, moreover, shy away from general education courses. Effort spent on them, they fear, will not advance their academic careers.

A prescription for producing a teacher ideally qualified to conduct a course dealing with non-Western countries might run in these terms:

Take a broad gauge professor now giving his entire attention to graduate students, or to advanced majors in economics, political science or history;

Let him spend several years in developing an area course for undergraduates, one which would be recognized as terminal and not as a preparation for future specialization;

Send him to his area for a stay of one or two years.

Without foundation support, few institutions could afford the investment described above. Foundations are already providing, at various university centers, post-graduate fellowships for the study of Asian, African, and other non-Western civilizations. Over a period of years, the fellowships will enlarge the supply of *experts* in these fields. But, as Ward Morehouse has pointed out, such fellowships will not necessarily enlarge *the supply of teachers equipped to conduct undergraduate courses.* This will occur only if the recipients find it worthwhile to turn their attention to the teaching of non-specialists. For this kind of teaching, the research centers will have to provide training programs which lay less emphasis than at present on language competence, and more on understanding economic characteristics, domestic politics, and foreign policy, and the interrelation of all these with cultural life.

Until the supply of properly trained teachers has been enlarged, colleges that wish to do more for the common run of undergraduate in the non-Western field will have to make optimum use of teaching resources immediately available on their own and neighboring campuses. They can free members of their own faculties from part of their teaching load to enable them to widen their knowledge of non-Western countries by extensive reading. Or, they can encourage attendance at one of the summer institutes for college teachers on Asia, Africa, Latin America, or the USSR.[17]

Neighboring colleges can pool their supply of faculty members having special knowledge of non-Western areas. A cooperative arrangement of this sort has been set up by four colleges in the Connecticut Valley: Mt. Holyoke, Smith, Amherst, and the University of Massachusetts. More economical use of combined teaching resources will make it possible for each of these colleges to expand its Asian and African course offerings. At the University of Massachusetts, four-college cooperation applies only to advanced students; but Mt. Holyoke, in addition to advanced work, will provide introductory courses open to freshmen and sophomores.

To introduce students to a broader understanding of non-Western areas is the goal of the joint program of Earlham and Antioch Colleges, established in 1959. The program involves the exchange of faculty members, and also a joint seminar in which teachers from both institutions are improving their knowledge of the music, philosophy, and religion of Far Eastern countries, as well as of their history and political institutions. The area studies given by four colleges in the vicinity of St. Paul, Minnesota, in cooperation with the Hill Reference Library, are designed for upper division students.

In September, 1960, a three-year program of Asian studies was set up to be offered jointly by Lynchburg College, Randolph-Macon Woman's College, and Sweet Briar College. The program comprises a course offered on each campus and a seminar for faculty members.

5. Courses in International Relations

In the early years of the present century, when courses in international relations were first introduced, they amounted to little more than lectures on current events, up-to-date diplomatic history. After World War I, teachers focused their attention on prospects for the preservation of world peace through the League of Nations. A more realistic approach was introduced in the 1930s by a group of scholars who identified power as the dominant factor in international relations. They found the pursuit of national interest—rather narrowly conceived by some—to be the dominant purpose of foreign policy.

World War II hastened a series of "transformations"[1] in world politics some of which had their origins well before that struggle. With the decline of the colonial powers, new national states emerged in southeast Asia and Africa. In older states, the making of foreign policy became a more democratic process. Epoch-making achievements in science and engineering introduced new problems in national defense.

To take due account of these and other changes, showing their significance for American foreign policy, poses a formidable task for teachers of college courses in international relations. Professor Swift has described their response to the challenge. "College courses today stress power and the complexity of world affairs rather than the state system: they probe deeper into the elements of national power, and in so doing take account of the theoretical and practical results of research in economics, psychology, and sociology. In debating the position of the realists and idealists and presenting the cold war, instructors now pay more attention to theoretical presuppositions; and in presenting accurately the picture of world politics today, they have had to give a larger place than ever before to Africa and Asia."[2]

Inevitably, the several hundred courses offered in American colleges vary widely in approach and emphasis. Some stress principles, others, rejecting abstractions, analyze *seriatim* the foreign relations of the major powers. The study of "transformations" is a new approach introduced with considerable success at San Francisco State College. Among the goals of instruction, training for citizenship still holds a prominent place, but few professors plead with missionary zeal for a particular brand of world organization or for a new program of American foreign policy. "Converting the unwashed isolationist masses to the secular religion of internationalism is not the dominant teaching goal of the international relations scholar."[3]

International relations is a required subject in only a few institutions; enrollments are apt to reflect the students' interest in foreign affairs. Thus, in private universities and liberal arts colleges which draw students from an upper middle class environment, the course attracts a larger proportion of the undergraduate body than in tax-supported institutions whose clientele has a more diverse and, in general, a less sophisticated background.

Enrollments

Our analysis of the academic records of 1,601 seniors in 34 representative colleges and universities[4] shows that only 130, about 8 percent, had taken a course in international relations at some stage in their college careers. (The selection of the sample of 36 institutions is described in Chapter 2. Two of the institutions gave no course in international relations.) Ninety-two percent graduated without having been exposed to the subject. In certain liberal arts colleges, Carleton and Oberlin, for example, where interest in foreign affairs has been traditionally at a high level, about 30 percent of the graduating class will have had the course. On the other hand, in some of the large state universities where the undergraduate body includes students in pre-professional schools—business administration, engineering, education, journalism, etc.—the proportion exposed will rarely exceed 5 percent.

Students' attitudes are not the only factor affecting enrollments. They depend also on decisions of the department of political science, or the department of international relations if one exists, on what kind of a course should be given and what students should be admitted. We are not concerned, here, with courses dealing with special aspects of international relations such as international organization, international law, international economic relations. Our interest is in courses whose titles —International Relations, International Politics, World Politics, and the like—imply a broader coverage. Should these courses be taught from the point of view of general education, admitting lower as well as upper division students, or should they be restricted to upper classmen who have a special interest in the field? On this point, marked differences of opinion have arisen.

Specialized vs General Courses

Some of the best known teachers think of international relations as a specialized subject which can be studied profitably only by well qualified juniors and seniors; until recently, this view determined departmental policies. A 1951–52 survey of the United States Office of Education[4] found that about two-thirds of all courses in social science departments relating to international affairs were designed for upperclassmen and graduate students. Freshmen and sophomores were excluded on the ground that they lacked the knowledge of history and the grounding in the principles of political science, which were considered essential to the understanding of international relations. This view is strongly held at the University of California, at both Berkeley and Los Angeles. From Berkeley, Professor Ernst Haas has written in a letter to the author:

In my mind, international relations is not an autonomous field, but an artificial compound of materials of social science disciplines and subdivisions of political science. I can more easily justify to myself teaching an introductory course in international relations—and we teach this course at Berkeley at a rather theoretical level, without explicit and systematic reference to current events or practical foreign policy problems—if my students have already been exposed to the mechanics of American government, comparative government, elementary economics, and at least American history. Unless I am sure they have already had this background, my interpretation of international relations could not be related in their minds to whatever else is important in a general social science context. Therefore, I would personally be both unwilling and unable to teach a course at the sophomore level.

A similar point of view has been expressed by Father Sellinger, Dean of the College of Arts and Sciences, Georgetown University:

Students who do not have a grounding in American history or

American government are ill-equipped to take courses which require considerable background in our own institutions as well as institutions overseas. It is precisely in these survey courses in international relations at the freshman and sophomore levels that one finds students developing the notion that one opinion is as good as another regardless of how well-informed any of the opinions may be.

Professor Arnold Wolfers, of the Johns Hopkins Washington Center of Foreign Policy Research, also has pointed out, in a letter to the author, certain dangers in teaching international relations below the junior year level:

If given to students with little background courses on international relations seem to me to have a curious tendency of turning themselves either into bull sessions on current events—as current as yesterday's newspaper—or being forced into the unpopular mould of sheer abstraction to which 90 percent of the students at that stage are thoroughly allergic. . . .

I have found it more fruitful for the students to take a course dealing with the major countries and regions first, and then to proceed to a generalized approach to international politics. But I should add that for years we followed the opposite course at Yale, and with satisfactory results, too.

Professor Hans J. Morgenthau of the University of Chicago does not agree with his distinguished colleagues. As a matter of principle, he sees no reason why basic problems of international relations should not be introduced into beginning courses. He writes:

I do not believe that factual knowledge concerning the world outside the United States is at all a prerequisite for the competent discussion of the basic problems of international relations.

However, emphasis is on the word "competent." You are, of course, well aware of the ease with which the field of international relations lends itself to dilletantic treatment. Such treatment can occur on all levels of instruction. In other words, what is important is to bring the students into contact with expert knowledge, and it seems to me to make little difference on what level that contact be established. In view of the absence of technical prerequisites, there is much to be said in favor of establishing such contact on the beginning level.

In an increasing number of colleges, international relations is taught as a general rather than a specialized subject. The University of Wisconsin offers a course for freshmen and sophomores. At the University of Virginia, the course in foreign affairs is open to second year students without prerequisites, ". . . purposely to afford a general education in Foreign Affairs for the general student." (Letter to the author from Dean W. L. Duren, Jr.) At Goucher, the course, which has no prerequisites, is designed for both the non-specialist and the potential specialist. The Political Science Department at Yale has recently changed its basic course to stress an awareness of world problems. The prerequisite in comparative government has been eliminated. The new course, which enrolls 500 students, is described in the catalog as "a study of competitive coexistence: the Communist challenge and the Western response—military, economic and political."

San Francisco State College has offered, since 1948, a one-semester general education course called International and Intercultural Relations. It is required of all four-year students who usually take it in the second half of the sophomore or first half of the junior year. (This requirement does not apply to transfer students. Hence, in graduating classes, approximately half will not have taken the course.) Eighty or ninety percent of them have had little or no knowledge of world affairs or of American foreign policy. Of this course, Professor H. H. Fisher has written:

I suppose for many teachers, especially the younger ones, it is more stimulating to deal with students who have had preparatory work in economics, political science, history, anthropology. Such students already have an interest in international affairs, but from the point of view of a liberal education and citizenship, these are not the ones who need instruction in this field most. The ones who need it most are those who have neither knowledge nor interest. For them prerequisites are not necessary but it is necessary to use instruction materials and method suited to their situation.

6. Professors in Uniform

Outside the framework of the academic curriculum, thousands of male students enrolled in the Reserve Officers Training Corps (ROTC) are receiving instruction by military officers in geography, American history, and international affairs. In the academic year 1959–60, about 260 thousand, one-seventh of all male undergraduates, were enrolled in ROTC units. The United States Army had 156 thousand cadets at 248 colleges and universities and the Air Force about 100 thousand at 175 institutions. The Navy ROTC enrolled 10 thousand students at 52 colleges. The Navy's program is voluntary, but in about two-thirds of the colleges where Army and Air Force units have been set up, ROTC training is compulsory for all able-bodied male students. Compulsion is the rule in practically all the land-grant colleges and in about half the state universities and privately-supported institutions.

Much opposition has developed to the compulsory feature of the ROTC programs. Students not interested in preparing for a military career resent the loss of time spent in drill, in laboratory work, and in the basic ROTC courses, for which they receive only partial academic credit. This negative attitude receives support from leading educators who believe that non-academic courses in the ROTC program interfere with the students' general and professional training. Student opposition, supported by faculty opinion, has recently caused the shift from compulsory to voluntary ROTC at a number of institutions, including Ohio State University, University of Wisconsin, Cornell, Rutgers, and Bucknell. Opinion in Washington is divided on the issue of compulsion. The Air Force, believing that with increasing college enrollments voluntary enlistment will provide all their officer requirements, seems willing to abandon compulsion. But the Department of the Army holds a contrary view.[1]

ROTC Programs and College Curricula

There is no single ROTC educational program but rather three programs—Army, Navy, and Air Force. Each service formulates and administers its own curriculum. Unification seems to have made no more progress on college campuses than in the Pentagon. The tripartite division is one of the factors that has prevented the integration of the educational efforts of the military with academic curricula. "The ROTC units . . . resemble foreign embassies within otherwise sovereign territories."[2] Commanding officers, it is true, are faculty members; colonels usually rank as professors. But their appointments stem from Washington, not from college authorities; their curricula are not subject to approval by college faculties; and their educational objectives are not necessarily consistent with those of the "host" institutions.

In all three ROTC programs, the students' work includes weekly drill, laboratory periods, and classroom exercises, the latter carrying either full or partial academic credit. The heavy traffic points, as in the academic curricula, are found in the introductory or basic courses offered in the first two years. (The compulsory feature applies only to these years.) Enrollments are much smaller in the advanced courses given in the third and fourth years where one finds only students aiming at officers' commissions. This is the rule both in institutions where ROTC is compulsory and in those where students volunteer. In colleges in which the basic two-year ROTC course is required, the drop in enrollment at the end of sophomore year is 50 or 60 percent. The number of survivors depends not only on students' choice but also on the standards of selection adopted by the ROTC commanders. At Indiana, recently, 500 freshmen were enrolled in the Army's ROTC unit. Of these, 250 *elected* to continue in the third and fourth years, in preparation for a second lieutenant's commission. But only 150 were chosen.

Opportunities to Learn about Foreign Affairs

In the Army's General Military Science curriculum, two courses or "blocks of instruction" afford students some opportunity to learn about foreign affairs. Freshmen take a course in American Military History (Military Science I) in which a substantial number of classroom hours are devoted to these topics: The Political Implications of World Wars I and II, The United Nations, The Cold War, and The Army as an Instrument of National Policy. In the sophomore year, Military Science III, The United States Army and Military Security, has a 10-hour unit which is designed to develop the students' understanding of the military threats to which the nation is exposed, the relation between military power and national security, and the role of the Army in limited war, conventional war, and total war. In the second semester of the second year of the advanced course (Military Science IV), much the same topics reappear. The recently announced revision of the Army's program is designed to lay more emphasis on general education and less on specialized training. Toward this end certain military subjects, such as instruction in weapons and marksmanship, will be taught in summer camps. The time thus released will be devoted to academic subjects—speech and writing, psychology, and political institutions. But the changes, it appears, will affect only the work of advanced students—juniors and seniors.

In the Air Force program, 20 "contact hours" of instruction in the first year are devoted to the Elements and Potentials of Air Power. (A contact hour is one hour of classroom work or drill. No academic credit is given for drill periods.) The course compares the American air force with those of the Soviet Union and its satellites, and with those of our allies in the Western world. Also, during the second year, courses in the Evolution of Aerial Warfare and Employment of Air Forces have some foreign affairs content. Much more is provided in specialized courses in International Relations and Military Aspects of World Political Geography. These courses formerly were taught to first and second year classes with large enrollments. But a new curriculum, adopted in 1958, but not fully effective until 1962, has transferred them to the senior year where they will be available only to the much smaller number of cadets who are preparing for commissions in the Air Force.

In the Navy's ROTC program, American Naval History occupies a large part of the first year. Examination of the textbook usually employed[3] indicates that the course is almost entirely concerned with the technique of naval operations.

In summary, ROTC programs contain only a few courses, where large numbers of cadets are enrolled, that contribute to the understanding of United States foreign policy or of the international scene. Air Force courses, which appear to be most promising in this respect, are available only to the relatively small numbers of advanced students who are working for commissions.

The Quality of Instruction

Grave misgivings have been expressed regarding the quality of ROTC instruction in non-military subjects. The officers assigned to ROTC units in general are competent in their own fields and are devoted to their task. But the educational experience of most of them has not provided adequate preparation for teaching courses outside those fields. Their brief assignments to ROTC units (1½ to 3 years) give them little opportunity for in-service training. Hence, ROTC courses in history, government, and international relations, as well as in engineering subjects, are conducted, in general, on a lower intellectual level than similar courses in the regular college curriculum. (Some of the textbooks seem to have been written for high school students.)

At The Ohio State University, a committee in charge of the Air Force ROTC Civilian Instructor Program observed that

. . . officers assigned to duty as AFROTC instructors are frequently handicapped by inadequate preparation in certain subject areas, by lack of experience and training in instruction and by general unfamiliarity with academic procedures; . . . their tours of duty are too short to permit them to acquire a professional competency comparable to that of their civilian colleagues and to become effectively integrated with the faculty of which they are nominally a part.[4]

It recommended that ". . . use of members of the regular academic faculty as instructors in the AFROTC be encouraged in every way possible. . . . that officers assigned to AFROTC be more carefully selected with regard to their preparation in subject areas in which they are to instruct and their interest in teaching; and that consideration be given to lengthening assignments to AFROTC duty, at least for key personnel."[5]

The lower level of ROTC courses in engineering subjects has given rise to criticism from the American Society for Engineering Education. Growing dissatisfaction with the quality of instruction in history and international relations has led, in a number of institutions, to arrangements whereby these courses are taught by members of the college faculty. At Harvard, a student can substitute a course in the Department of Government for a similar ROTC course. ROTC cadets at Yale can replace basic military science courses with courses taught in the Departments of History and Government. At Princeton, the Army has substituted a college course in the History of Military Affairs in Western Society Since the Eighteenth Century for its course in American Military History. At the University of Illinois, members of the college faculty have replaced military officers as instructors in the Air Force ROTC courses dealing with international relations.

INDOCTRINATION

The element of indoctrination, present in all ROTC courses, has given rise to much uneasiness in academic faculties. Indoctrination appears, in the efforts of the officers in each of the service units, to convert their cadets to a "service-oriented" point of view, and to exalt the role of the Army, the Navy, or the Air Force, as the case may be, in national defense. An avowed aim of the Air Force ROTC is to educate the youth of the country for "air age citizenship," bringing them to appreciate the importance of this branch of the armed services in preserving the security of the nation.

More disturbing is the seemingly unavoidable conflict of the emphasis on authority, inherent in all ROTC courses, with the spirit of free inquiry which the colleges cherish and try to encourage among students and faculty. The conflict is most apt to arise in the teaching of courses in history and international relations. The civilian instructor has been trained in graduate school to examine the sources, to sift the evidence, and to consider all relevant points of view before presenting his conclusions. Lacking this sort of training, the men in uniform are tempted either to avoid controversial issues or to lean heavily on what they take to be official opinion.

7. Natural Sciences and
   the Humanities

In all sectors of the college curriculum, an undergraduate may find courses which will contribute—either directly or indirectly, marginally or substantially—to his knowledge and understanding of foreign countries. In the natural sciences, he may find incidental mention of America's indebtedness to the work of foreign scientists. The best teachers of elementary physics will mention the contribution of Marie Curie, the French scientist of Polish origin, to our knowledge of radioactivity, and that of a Dane, Neils Bohr, to nuclear fission. In biology, they will acknowledge the work of an obscure Austrian priest, Gregor Mendel. Engineering students who have always regarded the automobile as an American achievement, will be surprised to learn of the pioneer work of three Germans—Diesel, Daimler, and Benz—on internal combustion engines and their application to overland transportation. Respect for English engineering progress will be heightened by knowledge of Frank Whittle's adaptaion of the jet engine to airplane propulsion. Hearing of Russian achievements in orbiting satellites in space may stimulate budding engineers to learn more about scientific work in that country.

In mathematics, the better teachers will awaken interest in foreign countries by referring to the development of arithmetic and algebra by the Hindus and later by the Arabs; by explaining how a Frenchman, Descartes, made analytical geometry more generally comprehensible by his invention of rectangular coordinates. They will make clear the indebtedness of all the natural sciences to Leibnitz, the German, and Newton, the Englishman, for their invention of differential and integral calculus.

Science and mathematics, Professor Redefer has observed, ". . . are international languages in themselves, and except for variations of when or how they are taught, they are much the same the world over. Algebraic equations look the same on the blackboards of Ceylon and Jordan, and chemistry laboratories smell the same in Israel and Lebanon."[1] But although the language of science is international, so that physicists and mathematicians have, in the past, freely exchanged ideas and information across national boundaries, considerations of national security now prevent, or restrict, their doing so. In discussing the causes of this change an instructor in mathematics or physics can introduce his students to a vital question of American foreign policy.

The fine arts and music transcend national boundaries, their appeal is universal. Studies in those fields, which not long ago were considered either as frills, or something to be pursued vocationally, now find a place in many institutions as integral parts of a liberal education. For example, as the result of newly revised distribution requirements, one finds many students at the University of California at Los Angeles enrolled in courses in the history and appreciation of art and music. To them, Italy acquires more meaning because of Michelangelo, Verdi, and Puccini; Germany is linked with Brahms and Wagner, and France with Debussy and Saint-Saëns.

In international relations where the phenomena of force and conflicts of values have such prominence, students can benefit greatly from the insights provided by courses in philosophy. Training in this field ought to guard them, on the one hand, from adopting a cynical attitude and, on the other, from seeking utopian solutions. Courses in comparative religions can show how people all over the world, seeking an explanation of the phenomenon of existence, or driven by fear and anxiety, strive to make contact with a supernatural power.

The Contribution of Literature

For major traffic points in the humanities, courses in which large numbers of undergraduates are enrolled, we have to look to literature and foreign languages. Two types of lower division courses give undergraduates opportunities to get acquainted with the literatures of foreign countries. The humanities sectors of general education programs in some colleges, notably at Harvard, Chicago and M.I.T., devote much attention to foreign literary masterpieces. Many college courses in freshman literature, European literature, and world literature require extensive reading in the works of foreign (usually European) novelists, poets, and dramatists. Now that excellent English translations are generally available, acquaintance with these works is no longer limited to the relatively small group of students who can read them in the original tongues. Hence, it is possible to list courses in literature among the requirements for graduation, with resulting large enrollments. At the University of Georgia, over one thousand sophomores are registered each year in a course in European literature; about the same number enroll in the world literature course at the University of Maryland.

Poets, dramatists, and novelists deal with universal human problems and emotions. From their writings, young Americans can learn that their hopes and fears, their joys and sorrows are not far different from those experienced by their contemporaries in Germany, France, and India, and that their conflicts and difficulties are in many respects the same. This knowledge tends to break down isolationist attitudes and to dispel ethnocentric prejudice. Professor Louise Rosenblatt has written:

Literature gives us concrete evidence of how differently men have phrased their lives in different societies. But literature, by its very nature, helps also to bridge those differences. For literature, which permits us to enter emotionally into other lives, can be viewed always as the expression of human beings who, in no matter how different the ways, are, like us, seeking the basic human satisfactions, experiencing the beauties and rigors of the natural world, meeting or resisting the demands of the society about them, and striving to live by their vision of what is important and desirable in life. Imaginative sharing of human experience through literature can thus be an emotionally cogent means of insight into human differences as part of a basic human unity.

Our delight in the picturesque or dramatic externals of foreign life, our interest in strange folkways, need not obscure our sense of the literary work as a crystallization of human emotions and aspirations, as a patterning of attitudes toward the world of man and nature. Sometimes these are explicit in the work, sometimes implicit, clothed in story and symbol. But always it is possible to reach through the literary work to the broader human patterns it reflects. Through the study of foreign literature, then, we are seeking to help our students to broaden their vision of the varied images of life, of the different patterns of values, of the contrasting habits of emotional response, that other peoples have created out of our common human potentialities. And these differences are to be seen as alternatives, beside which our way of life and our own system of values are to be placed.[2]

In the Department of English in the School of Education at New York University, the cultural approach to the teaching of literature is strongly marked. In a course called Literature and Human Values, 300 students each semester read and discuss European and English as well as American writers of the late nineteenth and early twentieth centuries. In a second course, European Life in Fiction, Professor Bogart, venturing outside the well-trodden paths of English, French, and Italian literature, introduces his students to Scandinavian, Polish, and Yugoslav authors, mostly of the nineteenth century. His purpose, as the title of the course implies, is to make the literature of those countries a gateway to the appreciation of their cultural ideals and accomplishments.

VOCATIONAL VALUES

Harlan Cleveland has stressed the vocational value of the study of foreign cultures, particularly the non-Western:

From the point of view of education for overseas service . . . the most important thing a liberal arts college can do is to teach its students how to understand a foreign culture. The best way to start is by learning about one culture alien to our own. With whatever deference may be due to Emile Gobineau, the racist, or Ellsworth Huntington, the physical geographer, the barriers between men today are mainly intellectual. To break the culture barrier one must learn to think differently—one must become aware of the ideologies and the patterns of thought that have developed over the centuries in another cultural tradition. For this understanding, art, literature, philosophy, and history are the core disciplines, at the expense of the other social sciences. Neither the politics of a country nor indeed its language can be understood by the foreigner who does not have some acquaintace with its intellectual traditions.[3]

Officials engaged in framing foreign policies, as well as those who administer them, can benefit from the study of foreign cultural achievements. Karl Deutsch has written: ". . . the student of literature or the humanities, and those practitioners of political and social science who approach the subject matter primarily in literary or humanistic terms, are most often the persons who make major contributions in the realm of qualitative analysis. They recognize new patterns that are just barely beginning to be dimly visible against the dark and chaotic background of miscellaneous, distracting and often trivial detail."[4]

The potential contribution of comprehensive courses in literature to the typical undergraduates' knowledge and understanding of foreign countries is undoubtedly great, but in most institutions of higher education, the actual contribution is much less. Among teachers of introductory courses in literature, relatively few are conscious of a sociological as well as an aesthetic purpose. Only a few feel an obligation to give their students an understanding of the culture of a foreign country as well as an appreciation of the beauty of its literary productions. The bulk of the profession—handicapped by lack of acquaintance with cultural anthropology, or indifferent to its implications for literature—follow the beaten path of historical surveys of American or English literature.

Foreign Languages

Beginning courses in three foreign languages—French, Spanish, and German—are major traffic points in the undergraduate curriculum. They attract more students than any other course except Freshman English. "Attract" is perhaps the wrong word; actually the big enrollments reflect requirements for graduation, rather than student preferences. About 70 percent of all institutions granting the B.S. degree have a language requirement *for graduation*, and more than 80 percent of those granting the B.A.[5] Those with no such requirement, for the most part, are small and inconspicuous institutions. The state of California is an exception, for the Board of Education, by a regulation adopted in April, 1951, and still in effect, expressly forbade any State College to require any foreign language as a condition of graduation. The Council of State College Presidents recommended the new regulation. In effect, it prohibits not only overall language requirements, but also all departmental requirements, in so far as their fulfillment constitutes a condition of graduation.[6]

This prohibition does not apply to junior colleges, private institutions, and the University of California—which is outside the jurisdiction of the State Board of Education. Some private institutions are laying great stress on foreign languages. Dean Smyth of the University of San Francisco, a private institution, writes:

For the past three years we have studied the question of the lack of proficiency of Americans in modern foreign languages. As a result of our study we have completely revised our approach to and teaching of language. Beginning with the Freshman Class of 1959 all students in the Colleges of Liberal Arts and Science must demonstrate a proficiency in reading, writing, speaking and understanding a language other than their own in order to graduate. (Letter to the author.)

NEGLECT IN SECONDARY SCHOOLS

In stressing foreign language proficiency, the colleges are striving to remedy a serious deficiency in their students' preparation in secondary schools, particularly in public high schools. In 1955, slightly over half of the nation's high schools offered instruction in one or more modern foreign languages. There were, of course, wide regional differences. In Connecticut, Maine, New Jersey, and Rhode Island, every high school offered at least one modern language, but only one-fourth of the schools in Arkansas, Iowa, Nebraska, North Dakota, South Dakota, and Oklahoma provided language courses. Returns from high schools in 41 states showed that, on the average, only one pupil in seven was receiving instruction in a modern foreign language; in seven states, only one in twenty-five.[7]

The admissions policies of institutions of higher education are responsible, in part, for the neglect of language teaching in secondary schools. Fifty years ago the typical liberal arts college required all entering students to pass examinations in French and German as well as Latin. At late as 1922, this was the policy of 70 percent of all institutions of higher learning. But, in the next 30 years, many colleges dropped the language requirement for admission. As a result, in 1957, this admission requirement was found in only 28 percent of institutions granting the B.A. degree and, in 1959, in only 23 percent of those granting the B.S. For this radical decline there were several causes. In the years between the two world wars, the prevailing isolationist attitude in large sections of the country condemned everything foreign. Also, at that time, educational goals were changing. The liberal education objective, to which languages were important, was giving way to increasing emphasis on vocational and pre-professional training.

REVIVED INTEREST IN FOREIGN LANGUAGES

After 1950, revived interest in the study of foreign languages was evident all across the country—in elementary schools, secondary schools, and colleges. The Second World War and the prolonged international tension which followed it were largely responsible for this change. The knowledge that the Russians were laying great emphasis on foreign languages, even in elementary grades, gave rise to "a spirit of frenetic emulation." Moreover, the colleges at this time were becoming increasingly aware of the cultural values of language study. To guard undergraduates against over-specialization in "practical" subjects, they required students to devote more attention to the humanities—particularly foreign languages and literature.

Thousands of students, anticipating the possibility of going abroad, began to appreciate the advantage of having some facility, however imperfect, in French, German, or Spanish. Acquaintance with foreign languages was coming to have vocational value, also. The sudden, widespread contacts of American officials and businessmen with their opposite numbers throughout the world revealed a shocking ignorance of foreign languages even among the supposedly well educated. Harlan Cleveland wrote: "What has really created a sense of national crisis in the language field is the discovery that most overseas Americans are not able to deal with foreigners in the local languages. For the first time in our history, language proficiency has indeed become a valid professional qualification for hundreds of thousands of Americans."[8] Congress belatedly recognized that, for effective conduct of foreign affairs, in government and in private business, language skills were essential. This was the basis for the federal subsidies made available in the National Defense Education Act of 1958.[9]

ENROLLMENTS IN LANGUAGE COURSES

In the fall of 1959, 693 colleges and universities reported enrollments of 390 thousand students in three major foreign languages—French, German, and Spanish. This figure, however, exaggerates undergraduate interest in foreign languages. It includes duplicate enrollments (some students take several

Table 5. COLLEGE ENROLLMENTS IN THREE MODERN LANGUAGES, 1952–59

(Percentage increases in fall enrollments over those of preceding year)

	1952	1953	1954	1955	1956	1957	1958	1959
Total College Enrollment	1.5	5.9	9.8	8.8	10.0	4.1	6.2	4.4
French Enrollment	2.7	4.7	4.3	7.0	6.5	3.7	11.1	9.4
Spanish Enrollment	3.3[a]	0.7	5.1	7.7	4.2	3.6	6.3	8.1
German Enrollment	5.1[a]	3.0	5.4	10.3	8.5	6.6	15.0	13.6

[a] Decrease in enrollment.

Source: Modern Language News, February, 1960.

language courses) and covers both graduate and undergraduate courses. Table 5 compares enrollment increases in the major foreign languages in successive years 1952–59 with increases in total enrollments in colleges and universities.

Over the eight-year period, when total college enrollments gained 58 percent, the rate of gain in the three major languages seems to have been only slightly less. In the years 1958 and 1959, however, the gain in the languages has been significantly greater than the gain in total enrollments. Increased interest in the study of German in these years has been particularly marked.[10]

Each year more young men and women are studying languages in college, and they are studying more languages. A few institutions offer courses in exotic languages spoken in the Far East, the Near East, and Southeast Asia—Chinese, Japanese, Hindi, Urdu, and Arabic; these are studied principally by graduates and advanced undergraduates. "The college student, if he is determined enough, *can* find a school that teaches Arabic or Russian, but his chances of finding a class in a major African language are practically *nil*."[11] The study of Russian has made striking advances. In the fall of 1957, the Appleton-Century-Crofts Survey found that 140 colleges and universities were giving one or more courses in the Russian language; in 1959, the number had risen to 296; and in 1960, to 480.

THE REVOLUTION IN LANGUAGE TEACHING

More significant than enrollment gains has been the introduction of new methods of instruction—particularly the aural-oral approach—with accompanying modifications in course content and in predominant educational goals. President Lyon of Pomona College has written, in a letter to the author:

In the modern European languages we have made great strides

in introducing students to the language, culture, and history of these countries by strengthening our faculty and by the development of a language laboratory which has been so successful that it has attracted attention throughout the United States. This advance in language instruction has been the most significant single thing we have done to introduce freshmen and sophomores to the culture of countries outside of the United States.

In fact, innovation seems to have been more active in modern languages in the past 10 or 15 years, and more promising of good results, than in any other branch of higher education. The new developments not only make the learning process easier but also tend to enlarge the contribution of language study to the students' acquaintance with the world outside the United States. It is true that the appreciation of foreign cultures, and understanding of the characteristic features of foreign civilizations, are not generally recognized as major goals by teachers of foreign languages at present. Most colleges give priority not only to developing the reading and speaking facilities of the students but also to acquainting them with the fundamentals of grammar. This is the traditional pattern: freshman courses stress pronunciation and grammar; sophomores begin to acquire facility in reading; conversation practice begins in the third year. Studies in foreign civilizations and cultures are reserved for a small group of the most advanced students, "the language majors." But the typical student takes only one or, at the most, two years of a language, usually just enough to satisfy degree requirements. Hence, in institutions where the traditional sequence of courses prevails, most undergraduates acquire from foreign language study a minimum of understanding of the distinctive characteristics of foreign peoples and of their outlook on life.

World War II, as we have observed, gave a strong impetus to modern language study. It was responsible for the introduction of new techniques, aural-oral and audio-visual, designed to make language teaching more effective by shortening the learning process. Many colleges where language laboratories were installed in the war years, have retained them, and their experience has stimulated others to experiment with the new methods. At present, according to Professor William Parker's estimate, these methods are utilized by language departments in some 200 institutions scattered across the country.

For at least a decade, teachers of foreign languages have discussed actively the virtues and defects of the new emphasis on listening and speaking. Approval and disapproval, it seems, depend a great deal on what one considers the primary goals of language learning. But on one point there seems general agreement: For rapidly acquiring comprehension of the spoken language and ability to communicate with foreigners, the aural-oral method surpasses the traditional grammar-translation approach. It has distinct vocational advantages, for example, for young men and women in a hurry to take jobs abroad. As to reading ability, there are wide differences of opinion. Enthusiasts, and there are many, claim that students who follow the new, natural sequence in language-learning— listening and speaking first, and then studying grammar and construction—eventually make faster progress in reading and translation than those who reverse the process. Hence, they arrive sooner at an appreciation of aesthetic and cultural values. At present, however, the conservative majority among language teachers continue to give reading ability precedence over oral facility. Supported by specialists in linguistics, they reject short and easy ways to language-learning; for them there is no substitute for grind, grind, grind.

Educators have long made much of the cultural values to be derived from language study. A nodding acquaintance with

French, and possibly German, they have always considered essential to a liberal education. But, today, language teachers are beginning to use "cultural" in a new, anthropological sense. They are recognizing that when young men and women acquire the ability to speak and understand a foreign language they possess a powerful implement for breaking through the cultural barriers which separate them from peoples in foreign countries. For many teachers, "cultural interpretation" has become an avowed aim, not a mere by-product of instruction.

Indications of a superficial cultural interest are usually found in the elementary textbooks. They contain colorful material illustrating characteristic features of the everyday life of Frenchmen, Germans, and Latin Americans. They describe what foreigners eat and drink; they depict the exotic costumes occasionally worn on feast days, and include some readings in folklore and history, usually without systematic arrangement. In 1953, a Seminar of the Modern Language Association (M.L.A.) reported that ". . . none of the existing texts attempts to present cultural insights in terms of linguistic structure."[12] "With few exceptions, texts of the 'cours de civilisation' type have as their primary aims a panoramic and encyclopedic representation of the factual data of a given culture."[13] Textbook descriptions of life in England, France, Belgium, Holland, and other Western European countries often read like the enthusiastic releases of national propaganda bureaus.

Against this type of acculturation, the M.L.A. Seminar, aided and abetted by social scientists, has protested vigorously. The significant differences, they contend, between American and foreign cultures are not to be found in geographical details, nor in piquant customs of dining and clothing, but in points of view, in values, and in attitudes toward life. For the Seminar, "significance" means relevance to international relations.

"Any misunderstanding between America and a foreign nation," they assert, "is more likely to center on a disagreement on values. . . . The bland travelogue that avoids such ticklish matters provides a conception of the foreign culture which the student may reject because of its obvious bias, or which he may accept until more extended experience disillusions him."

The Seminar's point of view has been approved by some of the best-known teachers. Professor Najam of Indiana University, writing of the goals of language instruction in a state university, holds that the cultural element is the "primary job." The main objective is to promote cultural contact with another literature and knowledge of another people through their literature.

Professor Peyre of Yale University has written: "The true problems facing international cooperation today are not economic or social, but psychological. The best key to their understanding and to their solution is the study of language and literature. . . . Only if we know another language besides our own, and if possible, several others, shall we be able to perceive what divides other people from us and also the basic similarities underlying such differences."[14]

At Purdue, several years ago, the language program was reorganized so as to take account of the needs of the forgotten man, the non-major who has to "pass-off" four semesters of a foreign language. In the reorganization, the assumption was adopted that ". . . language study can be a vital and liberating experience in itself, rather than a mere handmaiden to belleslettres. . . . The subject matter of the required courses became the contemporary civilization of the countries concerned, and the language practice was made primarily oral-auditory, rather than deaf and dumb."[15] Building the program around the use of audio-visual devices and the introduction of contemporary subject matter produced good results in terms of language knowledge. But Professor Hocking adds: "No less important in our opinion, are the gains in cultural understanding and in student attitude. Second-year students no longer fight their way through classics such as *Wilhelm Tell*, but they learn a good deal about recent and contemporary Germany and they find this to be worthwhile."[16]

ASPIRATION VS. REALIZATION. The reorientation of language teaching in the direction of socio-cultural goals is by no means complete. In most modern language departments, the culture concept is an aspiration rather than a reality. Students in elementary courses continue to spend their time mostly in drill, in attempting to master the mechanics of modern languages. Advanced courses, it is true, provide opportunities to become acquainted with foreign cultures through the study of literary masterpieces and the works of contemporary writers. But in such courses relatively small numbers of students are enrolled, mostly majors in modern languages. Insights into the ideals and the habits of mind of foreign peoples are not made available to the common run of student who rarely pursues language study beyond the second year of college.

Progress in making language study, for the bulk of students —those enrolled in elementary courses—an open gateway to foreign cultures encounters familiar obstacles. Conservative heads of departments, and there are many, oppose change. They are satisfied with the traditional methods and goals of instruction. Those who are willing to experiment have difficulty in obtaining funds for language laboratories, with their expensive electronic equipment, and in finding properly trained instructors. Relatively few language teachers have had more than a minimum of preparation in the social sciences, particularly in sociology and anthropology; others would be ineffective in conveying insights into foreign cultures to students.

The humanities bulk large in the educational experience of the common run of undergraduate in his first two years. From the point of view of foreign affairs, courses in this field, particularly in modern languages and literature, when taught by instructors who are alive to the cultural aspects of their subject, can have great significance. They serve to modify the parochial attitudes of young people who have come to college from small and relatively isolated communities, replacing suspicion of all things foreign with tolerance and, perhaps, friendly interest. Through humanistic studies, undergraduates may come to view people in foreign countries not as conglomerate masses but as individuals who are like themselves in many respects. Thus, perhaps, for the first time, they become imbued with a sense of the unity of mankind and aware of the common interests in peace and freedom which they share with all peoples.

8. College Curricula: The Need for Revision

The typical undergraduate is not well-informed on foreign affairs. When he emerges from college, his knowledge of foreign countries and his understanding of the basic principles and the current problems of American foreign policy are inadequate for the performance of his responsibilities, either as a plain citizen or as a community leader. His ignorance of the international scene is a handicap to possible employment abroad, either in public or private operations. Finally, it restricts his enjoyment of life as a liberally educated person.

In this and following chapters, we shall try to allocate responsibility for this grave deficiency in higher education and suggest remedies which seem appropriate. We shall look first at the organization and content of the undergraduate curriculum. Then we shall consider the posture of the students; how high do they rate knowledge of foreign affairs among the values of a college education? After that, we shall examine the attitudes of college teachers and administrators toward undergraduate education in this field.

Undergraduate courses of study are organized on a fairly

uniform pattern. In the early years of the present century, a great many colleges and universities, reacting against abuses in the prevailing system of free electives, adopted curricula founded on principles of distribution and concentration. By restricting the student's freedom to choose courses at will, they aimed to make sure that he acquired a certain amount of specialized knowledge in a single field, and at the same time obtained more than a passing acquaintance with other fields. In broad outline, the system of distribution and concentration operates as follows.[1] All the courses of instruction are grouped into three or four divisions, or fields of knowledge, each containing a number of interrelated departments of instruction. The usual classification is: natural sciences, social sciences, the humanities. The latter, a large and rather ill-defined group, comprises modern languages, literature, music, architecture, sculpture, painting and, in some cases, history, philosophy, and religion. In his first two years, the student is required to complete a prescribed number of courses in each field. In addition to these distribution requirements, there are general requirements applicable to all students. Freshmen, as a rule, are required to enroll in a course in English composition, and in most land-grant colleges all able-bodied male students must take two years of R.O.T.C. training, in either military science, air science, or naval science.

Before entering the upper division, at the end of the sophomore year, each student chooses a field or subject of concentration. In this field, his "major," he will be required to select advanced and specialized courses equivalent to about half of the work of junior and senior years, some 30 semester hours out of 60. The balance represent "free electives" which he is advised, in some colleges required, to distribute among courses outside his department or field of concentration.

For illustration, at Carleton College the required distribution is as follows:[2]

	Semester Hours
Rhetoric	3–6
Literature	3–6
Foreign Languages	0–14*
Biological Sciences	6–8
Physical Sciences	6–8
Social Science	6
Philosophy	6
Additional Distribution	6†
Field of Concentration	36
Total hours required for graduation	120

* Requirement may be reduced or eliminated by examination.
† Hours outside the division which includes the student's Field of Concentration.

Professor Schmidt wrote:

Distribution and concentration was a first step on the road back to unity. In the eyes of its proponents the process of disintegration growing out of complete freedom of election had been checked and a semblance of purpose and meaning restored. But for many this was not enough . . . The common cultural experience and the unified general education which the old classical college had at least tried to provide were still lacking. . . . The introductory courses in the three broad fields of learning were taught by the professors of the major departments, not as contributions to general culture, but as first courses in the major subjects.[3]

The search for a greater degree of unity in the undergraduate college program led to the introduction of the general education courses which we have discussed in Chapter 3.

College curricula today are composites of general and special courses. Beyond this statement, the only valid generalization is that they are constantly changing. Thoroughgoing revisions are infrequent because of the opposition of strongly entrenched, vested interests in the faculty and because of lack of agreement on the goals to be attained. (Reform of a college curriculum has been compared in difficulty to the task of moving a graveyard.) Minor changes, however, are constantly under discussion and are often adopted.

Fifty years of continual tinkering by curriculum committees have produced distribution and concentration requirements of baffling complexity. One finds in the pages of college catalogs qualifications and exceptions that rival the provisions of the federal income tax in their power to bewilder the uninitiated. To guide students through this maze of administrative regulations is one of the principal responsibilities of his counsellor.

To improve undergraduates' competence in international affairs, two types of reform in the curriculum have been suggested: (1) New courses might be introduced to inform the student about foreign countries, their history, their institutions, their culture, and their outlook on life. Also, courses which would teach him about American foreign policy and international relations in general. (2) Revision of existing courses, particularly introductory courses in world literature and modern languages, in history and the social sciences, is a frequently proposed alternative.

Harlan Cleveland has observed: "The habit of adding new courses, rather than analyzing how the old could be altered to accomplish a new purpose, is deeply ingrained in nearly every academic community."[4] Adding new courses is an obvious way of dealing with curricular deficiencies and is a relatively inexpensive operation. Even a whole new department, David Riesman has remarked, often costs less than a new dormitory or a hockey rink. Enthusiasm for adding new courses, however, has not been matched by any comparable drive to eliminate the old. The result has been described as "curriculum obesity." Many college curricula are cluttered with courses that have accumulated in haphazard fashion without systematic planning.

Opinions of Teachers and Administrators

In order to test academic opinion on the relative merits of adding new courses and revising those already established, the author, in June and September, 1959, addressed informal inquiries to administrative officers and faculty members in 225 colleges and universities in which he posed the following questions:

Should more courses dealing with foreign countries be made available to freshmen and sophomores? Should such courses be required of all candidates for bachelor's degrees?

What can be accomplished by the revision of courses already offered? Could they be modified so as to provide more knowledge and understanding of foreign countries?

A substantial majority of the 200 replies favored the revision of existing courses rather than the introduction of new ones. Some respondents remarked that there was no room in the lower division curriculum for more courses. Freshmen and sophomores already had their time fully occupied with "tool subjects and basic courses of the various disciplines." In institutions where studies in the first two years are rather rigidly prescribed in a core curriculum, it was observed that the injection of new courses would necessitate a major operation. Objection was raised to offering new courses dealing with foreign affairs *at the lower division level* on the ground that freshmen and sophomores were not sufficiently mature to deal with these subjects effectively. Typical statements are reproduced below:

From Dean Walter L. Riley of the University of Washington:

It seems doubtful that increasing formal offerings would solve the problem. Currently there are numerous courses available to our freshman and sophomore students in the Social Sciences and Humanities where they are introduced to a variety of comparative data and information of *foreign countries* and/or *areas*. However, the students are not required to take any of these and could so manage their academic programs to avoid any emphasis on other countries.

From Professor McKelvey of Occidental College:

The liberal arts college is today under some criticism for its tendency to proliferate courses. Thus the responsibility for enlarging student understanding of the world outside the United States would seem to have to be met through existing programs, improving them, making them more meaningful, and involving larger numbers of students in them.

From President Lyon of Pomona College:

I think the desired results can be obtained by modifying existing courses rather than offering new ones. An individual student is permitted to take only four or five courses a semester in an American college and we make a great mistake if we keep on adding new courses without thinking the whole educational program through. In fact, the practice of adding a course to meet a need, no matter how legitimate, in the long run so clutters up the curriculum that this and other objectives are often lost.

From Provost Neville of Lehigh University:

We recognize the importance of making all students more knowledgeable about international affairs. It would be very difficult, however, to introduce additional courses for this purpose as requirements for all students. The four-year curricula are already overcrowded with "essential" courses, especially for majors in science or engineering—a majority of our undergraduates. I believe that we can make further progress toward the objectives you indicate only by giving more emphasis to international matters in our existing courses—in all fields, science and engineering included. The first and essential step in this direction is to bring about a greater realization by all members of the faculty that the international view is of great significance in their fields.

From Dean Fjellman of Upsala College:

The advantage would seem to lie with the modification of content or method of teaching of courses now offered. In the social sciences this could probably be best done through a method of comparative study. In the humanities, comparative study could also prove useful. . . .

From Dean Simon of Western Reserve University:

I believe that it is not necessary to have a great many additional courses in international relations on the undergraduate level in our colleges. I think that we need courses in history, economics, political science and geography which stress fundamental principles and objectives. I believe that all of our students need to appreciate the interaction of historical, economic, political, and geographical forces in both domestic and international relations. If such emphasis can be given, I think that our students will be well oriented to the problems of foreign relations.

From Dean Arbaugh of Augustana College, Illinois:

I doubt whether more courses dealing with foreign countries should be made available to Freshmen and Sophomores in *our* college, at least extensively. Certainly I think no required courses should be added, for the program is already very full with science, foreign language, social studies, humanities and (in our case) religion.

From President Budd of St. Cloud State College (Minnesota):

I think that most of us actively engaged in the job of educating college age young people are aware of the tremendous need for increasing interest in foreign relations. I, for one, however, believe this is handled best as a concept pervading a number of courses or disciplines rather than as a separate course where one is very internationally minded for one semester and then forgets the whole thing.

From Professor Williamson of Louisiana State University:

I do not believe that the best approach . . . lies in singling out everything "foreign" for special study and dividing up our curricula in "national" and "international" subjects. Our best approach, in my opinion, consists in broadening and liberalizing *all* our courses by introducing in them all those contributions and aspects, regardless of source, which are relevant to the subject matter of the courses.

From Dean English of the University of Missouri:

We believe that we can best meet this need by reorganizing our present courses rather than by introducing new courses. The creation of new courses is not necessarily the most effective method of developing a program designed for a specialized objective. Better teaching, too, is more likely to result from a new approach within an existing course that has proved to be academically sound than from the substitution of an entirely new and untried course. This is not to suggest, however, that a new course should not be created when the need clearly exists.

From Dr. Lyle H. Lanier, Vice President and Provost at the University of Illinois:

In general, judging by our own College, I should think that more opportunities should be available for freshmen and sophomores to learn about foreign countries. Most of our courses and curricula of this type are open only to upper classmen and they usually are elected in rather small numbers. In order to be effectively available to freshmen and sophomores, such materials should be incorporated into courses which would meet the requirements in "general education" in the major areas of knowledge.

From Dean McDiarmid of the College of Science, Literature, and the Arts at the University of Minnesota:

Unfortunately it is true that many lower division students do not learn much about foreign countries or international relations. Nor can this deficiency often be repaired in the upper division because of the demands made upon students' time by specialized training. Certainly the immense increase in our international contacts and responsibilities at both public and private levels requires increasing sophistication with respect to other countries on the part of graduates, and it is probable that *the last chance to give such instruction to students en masse as distinct from specialists occurs in the freshman and sophomore years.* (Italics mine.)

From Dean Lichtenstein, Denison University:

I am intrigued by the possibility of radical revision of many existing courses. . . . beginning courses in political science, history, anthropology, and sociology, and I might add economics, philosophy, and religion, might well embody considerable material relating to foreign countries. In order for this to be done successfully faculty members must themselves become much better acquainted with foreign cultures. . . . For undergraduate education I am reasonably convinced that this approach may prove to be the most profitable one.

Arguments against introducing new courses are strengthened by financial pressures which in a number of liberal arts colleges have set in motion a trend toward *reduction* of course offerings. In order to economize teaching resources, selective pruning of the curriculum is being studied at three colleges—Westminster College, New Wilmington, Pennsylvania; Hastings College, Hastings, Nebraska; and Macalester College, St. Paul, Minnesota. Already one of them has reduced its course offerings from 560 to 450.[5] At other institutions, notably at Vassar and Notre Dame, curriculum reform has brought about a reduction in the number of courses required for graduation, the purpose being to give students opportunity for concentration on fewer subjects and for independent study. The tendency to reduce rather than expand the number of courses offered, or required, is in line with the renewed emphasis, particularly in colleges of liberal arts, on the values of a general education.

When New Courses Are Needed

On general grounds, a strong case can be made against the introduction of new courses. Nevertheless, in special circumstances they may be justified. In many of the smaller institutions, despite the progress recently made, there is real need for courses which afford the common run of undergraduate opportunity to study international relations and to learn about countries in Asia, Africa, and in other so-called non-Western areas. In the larger colleges where such courses are already established, more opportunities should be provided for non-specialists to participate. Professor Tucker of Johns Hopkins University writes:

Students should be able to take two types of courses, without being majors in a given field and without having to satisfy too many prerequisites. The one type of course should deal with the general problems of international relations and is best given within a political science department. To this may be added a course in contemporary international history. The other type of course should deal with separate countries or regions. They too should remain relatively free of prerequisites and not be aimed at the specialist or major.

It seems to me that universities should offer basic courses in the history, government and social structure of the Soviet Union, China, India and a number of other countries or areas. These courses should have few prerequisites and should be aimed at the undergraduate body generally.

Professor Roach of the University of Texas urges the creation of a new course in International Relations:

Ideally, it should be a two-semester course, offered at the freshman and sophomore level, and required of all students in the University.

I would regard approval for a one-semester course as a partial victory, and there would be some gain if the additional requirement was added only in Arts and Sciences although—as I noted above—the need is probably greater elsewhere. If the beginning student received this much exposure, it seems reasonable to expect that quite a larger number than do so at present would later elect related advanced courses.

Some educators do not accept curriculum obesity as a valid argument against the introduction of new courses where they are needed. These bold spirits have the temerity to suggest that courses bearing on foreign affairs, particularly those pertaining to the non-Western world, might be substituted for others of less importance. Dean Shirley of North Carolina State College wrote:

Certainly, the international complications of our time demand a thoroughly enlightened citizenry and I am sure that we could find in all curricula some courses which are of less significance than this particular objective.

This he gives as a personal opinion. He adds, "Yet, I doubt if the general faculty—certainly the ones teaching these questionable courses—would agree completely with me in this."

The same idea was vigorously expressed by Provost Eberle of the University of Chattanooga, who wrote:

It may be necessary to de-emphasize, if not abolish, more traditional courses the need for which, though it may still exist, is not nearly as great as the need for the study of new areas. It is always, of course, a painful process to sweep out of the curriculum the items that have outlived their usefulness. . . .

In general, I am opposed to the idea of always creating a new course or courses. However, at the same time I note that to create a new course seems the most efficient way to get the job done and, at the same time, to publicize the fact that something new has been added.

Suggestions such as these imply that in some institutions the education of the undergraduate in international affairs may involve not merely the revision of the content of courses but it may require a fresh look at the entire undergraduate curriculum. In an address at Bates College, Dr. Charles Phillips frankly faced this possibility. In considering how knowledge of Eastern countries could best be introduced into the curriculum he said, ". . . the answer is not to give just a few college students some understanding of the East, but to offer it to *all* our students." He countered the objection that there was too little time in the college program for Eastern studies by the remark that "[we must make] better use of what we already have. Essentially this means leaving out something we now teach, replacing it with material from the East." This he calls the creative way of reorganizing the curriculum, as opposed to the additive method.

Better preparation of students in secondary schools in the natural sciences and in history may facilitate revision of college curricula. If certain introductory courses were thus made unnecessary, a slot would be opened for new courses. "The History Department at Yale," according to a recent report, "anticipates a gradual withering away of the traditional survey approach because of improving high school training. . . ." Decreased enrollment in the survey courses in American history has been accompanied by increased enrollment in courses concerned with world affairs and non-Western countries.[6]

SHOULD NEW COURSES BE REQUIRED OR ELECTIVE?

Adding new courses open to freshmen and sophomores, a course in world affairs or in non-Western civilization for example, raises the question of enrollments. "The great problem is not reaching those students who *want* these subjects [international relations, foreign area studies, etc.]: it is reaching those whose major fields and distribution requirements leave them in almost complete ignorance of international and foreign affairs, particularly non-Western countries."[7] Obviously, if the aim is to enlarge the acquaintance of the average student with the international scene, the course is a failure unless it attracts a substantial enrollment. How can large enrollment be guaranteed? Should the course be elective, or should it be made a requirement for graduation, or is some compromise solution practicable?

Many administrators and teachers are either opposed to or skeptical about required courses; they believe that freedom stimulates effort and that compulsion provokes resistance. Students, they say, object to learning what they have to learn. There is danger, they believe, that the reaction against free electives may go too far; it may circumscribe too narrowly the students' freedom of choice. Already in many institutions, particularly in those that are tax-supported, all students are required, as a condition of graduation, to successfully complete courses in English composition and in American history and government, or to show proficiency in these subjects by examination. In liberal arts colleges, foreign language requirements for graduation are not unusual. In various types of institutions, either freshmen, or freshmen and sophomores, are required to enroll in courses in Western civilization or in similar general education courses. In addition to these regulations, departmental requirements limit still further the students' freedom of choosing courses. The result is that prescribed courses make up a large proportion of their total semester hours.

To our inquiry regarding required courses, Dean Roy of the University of Arizona replied:

Beyond the course in Western Civilization, I think it would be rather difficult to get any general agreement as to what other courses dealing with foreign countries might be required, particularly in schools where programs are highly departmentalized.

President Butterfield of Wesleyan University (Connecticut) wrote:

I think that in general courses open on an elective basis are the proper device. I am not much in favor of required courses in any area. It seems to me the cultural climate is so vital, varied and worldly that faculties have a hard time selecting what students ought to know. I think it is wiser, for this generation of students at any rate, to give them all sorts of varied opportunities. If the opportunities are there I have a hunch that large proportions of them are going to get some work in a culture outside their own.

Some support appeared in our correspondence for required courses in the general area of foreign affairs—courses in world geography, world politics, contemporary world history, foreign relations of the United States, and international relations. Professor Swift has urged that "some required course in world affairs is an indispensable part of liberal education in the twentieth century."[8] A few institutions, notably San Francisco State College, have introduced required courses in International Relations. Simpson College (Iowa) requires "basic study of Eastern as well as Western civilization to attain a degree." We have already mentioned the requirement in effect at New York State College of Education at New Paltz, that all students must enroll in a course on Asian civilization and in one on Africa and the Near East, and there are similar requirements at Michigan State University (Oakland) and the University of South Florida at Tampa.

Optional Distribution Requirements

The indifference of typical undergraduates to foreign affairs, which we have already noted, and which we shall presently discuss, gives little reason to believe that many would voluntarily choose new courses in this field. Students' unwillingness to elect courses in foreign affairs, on the one hand, and the faculty's reluctance to compel them, on the other, poses a dilemma from which *optional* distribution requirements may provide a means of escape. Many college curricula now require all freshmen and sophomores to complete a specified number of courses in each of several broad fields, *viz.*, humanities, natural sciences, social sciences. To fulfill their social science requirement, students may choose among introductory courses in economics, government, sociology, and in some cases psychology and geography. A similarly wide range of options is provided in the humanities. The inclusion of a course in international relations, or an area course, among the options in either or both of these fields might attract enrollments, especially if the student counsellors gave the courses their blessing.

9. Students and Faculty

In Ivy League colleges in the East and in liberal arts colleges in the Middle West and Far West which attract students from a sophisticated, upper middle class environment, keen interest in foreign affairs is the characteristic student attitude. This attitude is prevalent, also, in certain tax-supported institutions on both the East and West coasts where, because of highly selective admissions policies, students are strongly motivated and unusually intelligent. But where such favorable conditions are not present, students display little interest in foreign affairs. Indifference, at least in part, is the cause of the low enrollments in specialized courses dealing with the history, politics, cultural life, and economic conditions of foreign countries. (See Chapter 2.)

Students' Apathy

In a recent study, Fred Cole found that extreme apathy was the characteristic attitude of the bulk of students toward the study of international relations.[1] Dr. Cole's study dealt only with southern colleges, but apathy toward foreign affairs is not confined to the South. In a small liberal arts college in Iowa, the students have been described as "wholly allergic to the world outside their state." A professor at a well-known liberal arts college in upstate New York, when asked whether his students were interested in international relations, replied with an emphatic "No." He added that they showed little interest in anything outside their personal concerns. Indifference and lack of curiosity about foreign peoples, according to the president of a private university in the Middle West, are characteristic of his undergraduates. The dean of a woman's college in Virginia relates the apathy of students concerning foreign relations to their lack of interest in politics in general. Cynicism, rather than indifference, is the term used to describe students' attitudes toward international relations in a large state university in the Middle West. They regard foreign affairs as too complex to be understood by any but the experts. The issues are too big to be affected by the opinions of individual citizens. Contributing to apathy in foreign affairs is what David Riesman has called "this curious worldly parochialism of the young," their desire for security, which makes them cling to familiar surroundings, ideological as well as physical.

These observations are confirmed by an intensive study of the attitudes of several thousand students at 11 colleges and universities, conducted by Dr. Rose K. Goldsen and her colleagues in the Department of Sociology at Cornell Uiversity.[2] "Few students," Dr. Goldsen reported, "become deeply moved by anything political, or develop strong enough feelings about political occurrences to 'get worked up' over them."[3] In a later passage, she observes "The present generation of college students . . . is politically disinterested, apathetic, and conservative."[4]

A somewhat different view has been expressed by William C. DeVane, formerly Dean of Yale College. Describing the typical Yale undergraduate, he has written:

I think he is not apathetic in spite of charges of some of his hot-headed contemporaries and elders. He seems to me to be waiting for a flaming, clear cause, and has too many sympathies to take sides easily. Indeed, he has a deep well of skepticism in him—the advertisers, the psychologists, television quiz champions, and the politicians have seen to that. He has little faith in his world, and is inclined to say it is "a world he never made." He is far more inde-pendent of his family and traditions than his predecessor, but this also means that he is often insecure, unanchored and is sometimes security-mad.[5]

The undergraduate's lack of interest in foreign affairs is owing, in part, to the strength and variety of competing in-terests. A large proportion of students in their freshman and sophomore years devote most of their attention to athletics and social activities. Interpersonal relations loom large as the goal of their college careers. For the more serious-minded, particu-larly those who are working their way, vocational goals are uppermost. Even students who are not under financial pres-sure take the maximum number of courses in their major field.

The personal inclinations of college students or, more commonly, the persuasions of representatives of their major disciplines, cause them to elect more and more instruction from a single department or related field and less and less from the areas of knowledge remote from their specialty.[6]

To the average undergraduate, a course in non-Western civilizations, or in international relations, appears to have little or no vocational value. Few think of success in their future careers, as business executives, engineers, teachers in secondary schools, physicians, dentists, or lawyers, as in any way re-quiring knowledge of foreign affairs. Dr. Goldsen and her associates found that ". . . In the freshman and sophomore classes the opinion that vocational education should be the most important aim of college education takes precedence over all others."[7] Juniors pay more attention to general educational values; among seniors this goal predominates. For the purposes of this study, the changing climate of undergraduate opinion is significant. It may mean that many students' interest in public affairs, and particularly foreign affairs, is awakened too late. Their programs of study have already been fixed and opportunities to improve their acquaintance with the international scene have been lost.

Faculty Responsibility

Members of the departments of history and social science carry a heavy burden of responsibility for the average undergraduate's ignorance of the world outside the United States, and his lack of interest in American foreign policy and in international affairs. His teachers and the writers of his textbooks appear to have neglected rich opportunities, in introductory courses in history and the social sciences, in literature and foreign languages, to broaden and enrich his knowledge of world affairs. They have failed to recognize that for the bulk of the undergraduates these opportunities are presented almost exclusively in the survey courses usually taken in their freshman and sophomore years. Except for the relatively small group who choose to concentrate in history, government, sociology or economics, the introductory courses in these subjects also are *terminal*. This obviously holds true for the substantial number of young men and women, as many as 40 percent in some state universities, who drop out before the beginning of their junior year. (In institutions with a more selective admissions policy, the rate is much lower.) As for the four-year students, most of them in their junior and senior years will be too occupied with their major subjects to elect unrelated courses.

The typical college professor shows little concern for lower division students who are not potential majors in his own department. This is a hard saying, but it apparently holds true not only in history and the social sciences but in other fields as well. Members of college faculties, some by inclination and others in order to qualify for promotion, tend to give priority in their scale of values to research. They are less interested in establishing a reputation for successful teaching. It is only to be expected, therefore, that in dealing with undergraduates they devote particular attention to the relatively small group who give promise of research ability. They are likely to disregard the primary purpose of the introductory courses, which is to give the common run of student an over-all acquaintance with the subject matter as part of his general education. Instead, they look upon these courses only as stepping stones to advanced courses or, to change the figure of speech, as recruiting grounds for potential majors in their departments, some of whom may later qualify for advanced work in graduate school. Inevitably, the non-specialists, 85 or 90 percent of the undergraduates, recognize that they are being slighted and resent it. Instead of awakening their interest in his subject, the instructor, by concentrating on potential majors, may kill it.

Professor Richard Swift has observed that if in any department, political science, for example, the introductory course, neglecting the general student, is taught primarily as a means of preparing future specialists, it loses all claim to be listed as a requirement for graduation. He adds that "while it is perfectly legitimate for any department to use a course to try to attract majors, no department is justified in regarding as primarily for majors a course *all* students must take." (Letter to the author.)

It is in some measure owing to the warping of introductory

courses from their true purpose that they have failed to live up
to the hopes of their early sponsors. They fail, as presently
taught, to challenge the students' mental powers.[8] As a result,
many of the abler students who can afford to continue quit
college before the beginning of their junior year, a phenomenon which has caused concern in private as well as in tax-
supported institutions.

Among teachers of international relations, there is a division
of opinion regarding their responsibility to lower division
students. (See Chapter 5.) Some welcome to their classes
sophomores, and even freshmen, who have only a general interest in the subject. Others, seemingly interested only in
training an elite, hedge their courses about with prerequisites.
Often they admit only upperclassmen.

Programs of international studies usually are conducted for
the benefit of graduate students and advanced undergraduates.
Such programs do not, as a rule, aim to stimulate interest in
foreign affairs on the part of the common run of undergraduates, or to broaden their knowledge of the international scene.
In fact, the reverse may be true. Fred Cole reported that, in
Southern colleges "In one sense, at least . . . there is a more
explicit and broader assumption of responsibility for the non-
specializing student in the schools where there are no special
programs in international relations. Where some obligation for
increasing students' knowledge about international relations is
assumed by the institution, the responsibility necessarily is divided among representatives of several disciplines " (history
and political science, for example).[9] But in institutions with
specialized programs in international affairs, Dr. Cole found
that teachers outside the field tended to shift responsibility for
enlightening the average undergraduate to the very specialists
who showed little concern for him.

10. Summary and Recommendations

Making students more aware of foreign affairs involves more than the revision of certain courses or the addition of new ones; it involves, ultimately, changes in the attitudes of teachers and students, and in the climate of campus opinion. The task has even wider scope. It cannot be restricted to reforms at the undergraduate level; it involves American education at all levels. In the elementary grades, teachers will need to make greater efforts to stimulate curiosity about foreign lands and their peoples, and to induce tolerance for strange ways of life. The secondary schools need to do a much better job in preparing their students in American history and government, in world geography and world history. If students entering college had better training in these subjects, college teachers could pitch freshman and sophomore courses at a higher level, giving more emphasis to the interrelation of foreign and domestic affairs. Eventually, it might be advisable to drop the introductory lower division courses in American history and government from the college curriculum and to substitute for them, as optional distribution requirements, courses in comparative government, international relations, or non-Western civilization.

Reform of education at the graduate level is needed to improve the teaching of undergraduates in subjects related to foreign affairs. Prospective college teachers of history and the social sciences should be generalists and not mere specialists. They should be taught to view sympathetically the needs of the rank and file of undergraduates, particularly those in the lower division, and to regard instruction in introductory courses not as a bore but as a challenge.

Adult education, also, is involved. The interests and attitudes of freshmen and sophomores reflect those that characterize their homes and their local communities. Students whose parents and acquaintances are not interested in public affairs, and who are badly informed about events outside their immediate neighborhood, are less likely to show interest in foreign affairs than students from a less provincial environment. Here, we are concerned with what can be done to improve *undergraduate education*. Education at other levels lies outside our terms of reference. It is important, however, to recognize that progress at the undergraduate level will always be related to progress at other levels.

The wide diversity of American colleges and universities, in size and resources, in academic standards, and in the qualifications of their students, makes it impracticable to frame a set of uniform recommendations for the improvement of undergraduate education in foreign affairs, or in any other field. Instead, the following pages suggest various lines of policy and avenues of approach which may be helpful to administrators and faculty members who want to do a better job in educating the common run of undergraduates in foreign affairs.

SPECIALIZED COURSES

Small enrollments in specialized courses dealing with foreign affairs are largely the result of students' lack of interest in the subject. To remedy this situation, to convert indifference into active concern is a long range task which we shall consider later. Faculty regulations also restrict enrollments by refusing admission to students who have failed to take one or more prerequisite courses. Such regulations, in every college, should be examined with care, and some skepticism, by the Curriculum Committee, to see whether courses now restricted to upper division students might not profitably be opened to sophomores, or in some cases to freshmen as well. No instructor should set up new prerequisites except with the permission of the committee.

Inadequate counselling is in part responsible for low enrollments in elective courses dealing with foreign affairs. Freshmen and sophomores know little about the curriculum. They are not acquainted with the content of upper division courses, particularly in subjects not directly related to their special interests. Here is a new opportunity for the counsellor. At present, he helps students with personal problems and tries to ease their "adjustment" to college life. He interprets, for them, the complex provisions of the college catalog so that they shall not fail to meet all the requirements and acquire all the credits necessary for graduation. He guides them in the choice of courses allied to their vocational interests. However, giving advice on courses from the point of view of their contribution to the students' general education usually is not regarded as one of his responsibilities. By including this service among the counsellor's duties, colleges would increase enrollments in underpopulated courses, making more effective use of teaching resources, and at the same time improve the chances that seniors will emerge better informed about the world around them and better prepared for responsible citizenship.

GENERAL EDUCATIONAL COURSES

Whatever knowledge and understanding the bulk of students acquire about foreign affairs, they will probably get in introductory, lower division courses. Deans and heads of departments, therefore, should take a fresh look at the content of these courses to find what changes could be made which would enlarge the students' acquaintance with the international scene and, at the same time, make instruction in the subject matter itself more effective.

HISTORY AND THE SOCIAL SCIENCES. At present, in most colleges and universities, introductory courses in American history and the social sciences are badly in need of reorganization. American history is isolated from world history; the first course in government deals almost exclusively with the government of the United States; the descriptive sections of elementary economics consider only the American economy. Introduction to sociology devotes attention almost exclusively to American social conditions and American social problems. Concentration on the American scene in these courses deprives the student of knowledge of the history, the political institutions, and economic and social conditions in foreign countries. Likewise, it is bad pedagogy, for it neglects opportunities to deepen, through comparison and contrast, the students' understanding of American institutions and American policies.

Courses in the history of Western civilization provide for many undergraduates, particularly in schools of business administration and in teachers' colleges, their principal source of information on foreign countries. Courses in this field which superficially treat a vast range of historical events should be revised so as to provide more intensive consideration of selected topics or epochs.

Courses in Western civilization usually fail to deal with the USSR and countries in Asia, Africa, and Latin America. In the present overextended condition of these courses, injections of non-Western material seems inadvisable. It seems preferable to deal with non-Western civilizations either separately or in a course on world civilization.

Even better results, the author believes, might be obtained by supplementing the survey course in Western civilization, or world civilization, with one or more courses giving concentrated attention to a non-Western area. Because competent teachers of non-Western civilizations are in short supply, colleges, before setting up new courses, should explore the possibilities of utilizing the teaching resources of neighboring institutions, through cooperative arrangements.

INTERNATIONAL RELATIONS

All colleges should make available to lower division students a course, or courses, dealing in fundamental fashion with problems of American foreign policy, the causes of international conflicts, and the means of avoiding or alleviating them.

R.O.T.C. COURSES

In R.O.T.C. courses dealing with American history and international relations, in general, instruction is conducted at a lower level than in corresponding courses of academic programs. In courses taught by military officers, a certain amount of indoctrination seems unavoidable. Consequently, these non-military subjects should be taught by civilians, regularly appointed members of college and university faculties who are responsible to academic authorities.

LITERATURE AND LANGUAGES

Teachers should exploit more fully, for the benefit of the common run of undergraduates, the rich contributions which modern literature and languages can make to the knowledge of foreign countries. These courses should serve as a gateway to the understanding of foreign cultures. For effective work of this sort, teachers will require more training than they now receive in cultural anthropology and sociology.

THE QUALITY OF INSTRUCTION

For general education courses, the highest type of instruction should be provided. They should not be staffed, as so often happens at present, principally by graduate assistants and the less experienced junior members of the staff. For freshmen and sophomores, the most valuable end-product of an introductory course will not be a collection of facts but the command of a few sound generalizations and a useful method of approach to a social science. This kind of instruction can be supplied only by the best teachers. To economize their services, departments should experiment with recently devised electronic aids, including closed-circuit television.

Unfortunately, at present, successful teaching of introductory courses is not as likely to advance a young instructor or assistant professor as research and publication. Hence, in order to guarantee a continuous supply of good teachers in the lower division, administrative officers may have to revise their criteria for promotion.

EXTRACURRICULAR PROGRAMS

Although extracurricular activities were not included in this study's terms of reference, their relation to work in courses deserves attention.

College authorities who are seriously interested in giving the bulk of their undergraduates a sound basis for understanding foreign affairs should devote their time and energy primarily to reforms within the curriculum. Extracurricular activities have a higher advertising value and are easier to set in motion, but the results are less substantial. Too often such activities have ". . . a rather sentimental quality. They tend to further the notion that international relations are chiefly a matter of good-will and emotional commitment."[1]

Extracurricular programs may usefully supplement classroom work and independent study, but are no substitute for either. A lecture by a foreign diplomat or a United States Foreign Service officer may provide "a quick injection of information and interest" (to quote Professor Byrnes) but will have little lasting value unless coordinated with classroom work.

For the most part, the students who attend the various meetings, visit the exhibits of foreign art, attend the showings of foreign films, and go on field trips to Washington or to the UN headquarters in New York are majors in political science, history, or international relations. Although the common run of undergraduates may rarely participate in these activities, they, nevertheless, may serve to make him more aware of, and more interested in, what goes on outside the United States. They may help to create on the campus a climate of opinion favorable to the study of foreign affairs. This is one of the chief functions of the International Relations Clubs that are active on some 200 campuses.

The effectiveness of extracurricular activities in supplementing classroom instruction and in stirring the undergraduates' interest varies widely from one campus to another. As a rule, it is at a maximum in institutions where, *within the curriculum,* courses dealing with foreign affairs are best organized and where they attract the largest relative enrollments. In such cases where intra- and extracurricular programs reinforce each other, it is not always easy to locate the initial impetus. In fact, both may have had a common origin. Unusually widespread interest in foreign affairs among the undergraduates in some colleges often has been owing to the energetic efforts of a single officer—a dean or a president—whose experience in war or in postwar government service abroad convinced him of the need of giving all undergraduates more knowledge of foreign countries and their relations with the United States. In certain church-related Protestant colleges and in a number of Roman Catholic institutions, a strong missionary interest among both students and faculty explains the exceptional attention to non-Western countries in the curriculum and in extracurricular activities.

Each year some 3,500 undergraduates receive academic credit in American colleges and universities for study in foreign universities, either in summer courses, in Junior Year Abroad programs, or in independent study.[2] Under the best conditions, the foreign experience can make a unique contribution to the participating students' knowledge of foreign countries. It can make them more competent in foreign languages, can deepen their appreciation of the characteristic features of foreign cultures, and stimulate them to vigorously pursue studies in foreign affairs on their return to their home campuses. At some universities, notably at Stanford, careful selection of the students who participate and systematic organization and supervision of their foreign studies have enabled students to realize all these advantages. Elsewhere, the results have proved far less satisfactory. "Too many of the programs for study or work abroad have been shallow in conception and shoddy in execution, leading at best to a gloss of cosmopolitanism to adorn the traveler and at worst to the false belief that he has acquired more than a superficial notion of what the world is all about."[3]

Like extracurricular activities, the study abroad programs (co-curricular, if you like) have minimal importance in the foreign affairs education of the common run of undergraduate. Both the expense of travel and the lack of interest restrict student participation in most institutions to a small fraction of the undergraduate body. The Stanford program enlists each year only 280 out of a total enrollment of 5,000 undergraduates. At Kalamazoo College, where a Summer Study Abroad program has recently received a $1,600,000 endowment, President Hicks expects that ultimately one-half of each year's senior class will have studied abroad. But these figures are exceptional; taking the country as a whole, only one undergraduate in a thousand benefits from foreign study programs.

A COORDINATOR OF STUDIES AND ACTIVITIES

The failure of the colleges to give their undergraduates adequate knowledge of the international scene, and the problems which confront the President in the field of foreign policy, is not so much due to the lack of resources as to the failure to effectively employ available resources.

In every college and university, therefore, the president should assign to a senior professor, or to a senior member of his administrative staff, the duty of coordinating curricular and extracurricular activities relating to foreign affairs, so that they may be more effective in undergraduate education.[4] The person so designated, who might be known as the Coordinator of Foreign Studies, should, of course, have no authority to determine what should be taught, by whom, or how. Nor should he be able to determine the direction of research. He should "coordinate" in the true sense of the word, bringing various activities into harmonious relation with each other. The ways in which he will carry out his assignment in any institution will vary with local circumstances. Here, we can only outline the general nature of his task.

At the outset, he should make an inventory of the college's resources for education in foreign affairs. He should make himself acquainted with the content of courses in various college departments and in schools of the university which contribute, or which might contribute, to the undergraduate's knowledge and understanding of the international scene. From the same point of view, he should study extracurricular activities and include them in his inventory. Every college has on its teaching staff a number of men and women—they may be anthropologists, biologists, or specialists in public health or in municipal administration, or economists, or engineers—who have lived, worked, and traveled abroad. The knowledge they acquired constitutes one of the institution's resources for the study of foreign affairs. In most cases, this fund of information and opinion, because it is dispersed, is not fully exploited. It should be one of the duties of the Coordinator to be informed about faculty members' foreign experience so that at appropriate times and places, perhaps in general education courses, or in students' discussion groups, they can make useful contributions.

Every college, except the smallest and the poorest, offers in its various fields of study—in history, in the social sciences, and in the humanities—eight, ten, or a dozen specialized courses which aim to provide either knowledge of foreign countries, or of American foreign policy, or both. But, as we have seen, such direct exposure courses attract few undergraduates. Working through student counsellors, the Coordinator should attempt to make sure that failure to enroll in these courses is not owing to the lack of information about them.

General education courses, the chief traffic points in the undergraduate curriculum, offer students opportunities for instruction in foreign affairs, but they are usually oriented to the American scene. Here the Coordinator faces a delicate task. He cannot impose his ideas on his colleagues. He can, however, endeavor to make clear to them that giving a wider orientation to their courses would enhance their educational value.

The non-specialist undergraduate is not attracted by lectures, forums, exhibits, and international relations clubs or other extracurricular activities designed to stir interest in foreign affairs. He makes few contacts with students from foreign countries. Here is another job for the Coordinator. He should attempt to establish closer connections between the curriculum and extracurricular activities, and should be on the lookout for ways by which the foreign students might be brought into contact with a larger number of undergraduates.

Professors of history, political science, and economics take responsibility for the education of students who have a special interest in foreign affairs. But no one takes responsibility for the non-specialist, to make sure that knowledge of foreign affairs forms a part of his general education. Looking after this forgotten man should be a prime responsibility of the Coordinator. In this task, he must look to the student counsellors to help him. Without having formal jurisdiction, the Coordinator should be in a position to advise these advisers. To make their services to undergraduates more effective, he should furnish them the information which he has assembled on courses dealing directly with foreign affairs.

Programs of international studies which, ideally, should radiate interest in foreign affairs throughout the campus community, are now often insulated from it. To find a remedy for this situation should be one of the tasks of the Coordinator. He should endeavor to throw bridges across the gap which, in many colleges and universities, separates specialized education from general education in foreign affairs.

The apathy of the typical undergraduate—his indifference to matters of public policy—presents a formidable obstacle to his education in foreign affairs. To transform apathy into interest and indifference into concern, should be one of the Coordinator's principal preoccupations. Students are sensitive to the prevailing climate of campus opinion. They want to do what is being done, to say what is being said, and to believe what is believed. If, in the campus atmosphere, they continually detect indications of interest in foreign affairs they, too, will become interested. The establishment, perhaps in the graduate school, of a new program of international studies, if well publicized, or the appointment to the faculty of a distinguished British or Italian historian, or an eminent foreign scientist or a celebrated poet, will attract undergraduate attention. By adding a bit of drama to the arrival of a group of students from India, Russia, or Africa, or to the departure of fellow students for a year of foreign study and travel, the air of the campus could be impregnated with extra-American elements.

The 50,000 students from abroad now enrolled in American colleges, universities, and technical schools represent a neglected source of knowledge and understanding of foreign countries. The almost universal failure, to date, to effectively utilize this resource has several explanations. About one-half the men and women from abroad are either graduate or special students and are more mature than the average American undergraduate. Foreign students are usually housed off-campus; in their studies, they are associated principally with professors and graduate students. The few undergraduates who seek them out are usually specializing in some aspect of foreign affairs. In spite of these and other obstacles, several women's colleges, among them Sarah Lawrence and Wellesley, and a few co-educational institutions, notably the University of Arizona, University of Minnesota, and Ball State Teachers College, have achieved some success in making foreign students acquainted with a fairly large number of undergraduates, to their mutual benefit. The Coordinator should study procedures of these institutions to determine whether they might be adapted or improved in his institution.

Stirring undergraduates' interest in foreign countries is not a one-man job. To achieve substantial progress in this direction, the Coordinator will need day-by-day assistance, not only from teachers of courses in international relations but also, and more importantly, from teachers of history and geography, government, economics and sociology, languages and literature, religion and philosophy. In their introductory courses, particularly, they should be on the alert to enrich instruction by relevant comparison of American life with foreign institutions, traditions, and philosophies. Thus, many of the Coordinator's colleagues will share responsibility with him for making American college students constantly aware of peoples in other parts of the globe whose interests and theirs are interdependent. Dean Watts, of Brown University, has written:

What really matters is to establish on a given campus, in all courses where it can find expression, an intellectual atmosphere which assumes our deep involvement with countries outside the United States and outside the centers of Western culture. The sensitivity of the faculty to such matters is what counts. (Letter to the author.)

. . .

The theme of this book is that knowledge and understanding of the international scene should form an integral part of the education of all college undergraduates. We have argued that young men and women emerging from college need acquaintance with foreign affairs if they are to speak and act intelligently and responsibly as voters and citizens. Furthermore, they need this sort of knowledge to enable them to fully enjoy life as intelligent persons. From the second point of view, the purposes of the study of foreign affairs are identical with those of a liberal education, i.e., education for its own sake— ". . . to know the sheer joy of understanding; to speculate, to analyze, to compare, and to imagine."[5]

These two objectives need not conflict; each can supplement the other. There is no reason why a student who, in order to better discharge his civic responsibilities, has taken courses relating to foreign countries, may not also derive from them keen intellectual enjoyment. Conversely, a student who has studied international affairs to round out his general education, or out of pure intellectual curiosity, will find knowledge thus acquired valuable in forming intelligent judgments on issues of foreign policy.

This book has focused attention on the common run of undergraduate. It has emphasized his need for knowledge of foreign affairs and has pointed out various ways in which colleges and universities can satisfy that need. By this emphasis, however, we do not intend to depreciate the value of specialized studies at the undergraduate level. The country needs more men and women whose expert knowledge in foreign affairs fits them for teaching and research, and for positions in private industry and government employment. Likewise, it needs legislators and men of affairs whose accurate and comprehensive knowledge of the international scene enables them to speak with wisdom and authority on issues of foreign policy. The need for an elite—well-qualified leaders of opinion on questions of foreign policy—is well recognized. To satisfy this need, colleges and universities, aided by foundation grants, are putting forth vigorous and, on the whole, well-directed efforts. But in their concern for the leaders they have neglected the followers.

Now they need to recognize that leaders are powerless without followers, and that the quality and effectiveness of leadership in foreign policy will in large measure depend on the response of educated public opinion. The followers must not be an ignorant crowd, giving unquestioning assent to policies enunciated by their leaders. They must include a substantial body of well-informed men and women genuinely interested in foreign affairs who will support only the policies which they can defend with a good conscience, and who will bring pressure on the leaders to modify or abandon policies which fail to meet this test. To increase the number of followers of this type, and to strengthen their influence, should be one of the major purposes of general education in foreign affairs.

Appendix A. A Test on Foreign Affairs

The Test on Foreign Affairs was designed to determine how much young men and women about to receive their bachelor's degrees from American colleges and universities know about foreign affairs. The questions not only probed their stock of information but also attempted to test their understanding of the interrelations among the facts at their command, and their significance. This was a test of achievement, not of capacity for original thought.

For assistance in the selection of questions, we appealed to 200 men and women with broad knowledge of world affairs, asking each to suggest five questions which would test knowledge and understanding of the international scene. Their questions, we specified, should be designed for the common run of undergraduate—young men and women who were planning careers in business, engineering, education, law, medicine, the ministry, or as housewives—and *not for students who had specialized in international relations.* Other specifications were: (1) the questions. should explore the students' knowledge in a variety of fields, in geography and natural resources, the history, government, and the economic organization of foreign countries, also international relations and American foreign policy; and (2) the questions should concern matters of more than passing significance. They should refer to persons, events, and conditions which had been considered important over a period of at least five years and which would probably continue to be so regarded for five years to come. In other words, this was not to be a test of students' ability to recall tidbits of information on current events.

Over 100 well-known educators, business and professional men, scientists, and persons with experience in public affairs on national and international levels sent in lists of questions containing several hundred different items. (A list of the contributors will be found in Appendix C.) From this wealth of suggestions, the Educational Testing Service (E.T.S.) prepared a test, consisting of the 80 four-choice questions. In its task, the E.T.S. took account of the relative emphasis given by the panel members to information of an economic, historical, political, or geographical nature, and also to knowledge of various regions—the Far East, Latin America, Russia, etc. To test not only the students' power to recall facts but also their ability to put facts together in a meaningful pattern, E.T.S. made extensive use of maps, charts, cartoons, and brief excerpts from important documents. To correctly answer questions based on this material, the students had to draw inferences and apply facts in specified situations.

The test was administered in May–June, 1960, to 1,958 seniors in 175 colleges and universities.[1] This sample represents a rough cross section of the accredited institutions in the principal regions of the country. Within each type and region, we selected typical institutions, taking account of size, scholastic standards, and other characteristics. Selection was based on information obtained from college catalogs and directories of institutions of higher learning, supplemented by interviews with administrators and teachers in 40 institutions, and by extensive correspondence. Tentative lists were submitted to well-informed educators and then revised in the light of their opinions. Although this procedure gave less than proportionate representation, numerically, to institutions that are not well-known, including many with a low academic rating, it was considered, nevertheless, more suitable for the present study than one which would have required elaborate statistical apparatus. The sample thus constructed included 46 state universities, 29 private universities, 36 complex colleges, 7 technical schools, 7 teachers colleges, and 50 colleges of liberal arts. Represented within the 175 institutions were 69 schools of business, 79 schools of education, 56 schools of engineering and 131 schools of liberal arts.[2]

At each school, five to eight students took the test. They were selected at random, according to detailed instructions furnished by the E.T.S.

The Results

Looking at the performance of the whole group of seniors, we find that, on the average, they were able to answer correctly only 55 percent of the questions—44 out of 80.[3] The lowest scores were registered by a few students who got only 15 right answers. At the top was a single student in business administration at the University of Texas, who got 77 right. Seventy-five percent of the students answered less than 53 questions correctly. The lower 25 percent had less than 36 right answers. The score distribution is shown in Figure 5.

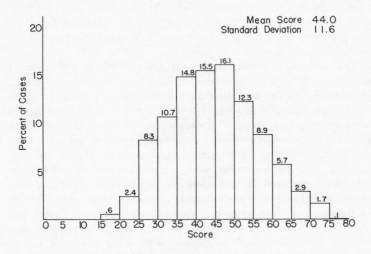

Fig. 5.   Score distribution for total group of 1,854 seniors

ANALYSIS BY CURRICULA

Table 6 indicates that students enrolled in engineering and in liberal arts curricula had more knowledge of foreign affairs—assuming that the test was valid for this purpose—than students preparing for careers in business or education. Judging by their average scores, the engineering students, it may appear, are better informed than those in liberal arts, but the difference is not significant.[4] The gap, however, is significant between the performance of the engineers and the liberal arts students, on the one hand, and business and education students on the other. Business school students, it will be observed, turned in a considerably better performance than the young men and women who were preparing to be teachers.

Table 6. ANALYSIS OF SCORES BY CURRICULA

Curriculum	Number of Cases	Mean Scores		Range of Scores[a]
Engineering	407	47.4[a]	59.3[b]	17–72
Liberal Arts	581	46.6[a]	58.3[b]	15–75
Business	452	42.7[a]	53.4[b]	17–77
Education	414	38.8[a]	48.5[b]	15–70

[a] Average number of questions answered correctly.
[b] Average percent of questions answered correctly.

The ranking of the four curricular groups on most of the individual questions was the same as on the whole test. On almost every one of the 80 questions, the percentage of liberal arts and engineering students who answered correctly was greater than that of students in the other curricula.

The differences in the average scores of students in the various fields of concentration correspond only roughly to the differences in their exposure to courses affording knowledge of foreign affairs. Analysis of academic records in Chapter 2 showed that liberal arts students took more courses dealing with foreign affairs than students in any other major curricular group; liberal arts students also scored high in the test. At the other end of the scale, students in schools of education showed the least knowledge about foreign affairs. Their transcripts also showed that they ranked low in Direct Exposure. (See Table 2.) In both performance and in exposure, students in business administration occupied a middle position between liberal arts students and those in education.

Our analysis of the academic records of 266 students in engineering curricula showed that 125, almost one-half the total, had taken no courses in any subject directly related to foreign affairs. Yet, engineering seniors made high average scores on the Test on Foreign Affairs. For this apparent anomaly, there are two possible explanations: (1) Engineering curricula attract students who are more capable than those who are preparing for careers in business or teaching. Evidence on this point is supplied by the results of scholastic aptitude tests under the Selective Service College Qualification Test Program.[5] (2) The high standards of performance demanded in engineering schools eliminate the less fit and develop mental alertness among those that survive the four-year course. Thus it may be that engineering seniors in our sample learned more about foreign affairs from extracurricular sources than students in other fields.

The low ranking of business school seniors in the Test on Foreign Affairs, also, may be related to their academic standards. Most of the undergraduate schools do not pursue selective admissions policies nor do they screen their students rigorously at the end of freshman or sophomore years.[6]

SCORES OF THREE GROUPS OF LIBERAL ARTS STUDENTS[7]

Table 7 compares the performance of the three groups of liberal arts students. The significantly higher average scores of the social science students result, in part at least, from the presence of majors in history and political science, who regularly include in their programs courses dealing with foreign affairs. No significant difference separated the average scores of students in the natural sciences from those in the humanities.

ANALYSIS BY TYPES OF INSTITUTIONS[8]

Seniors in private universities made a better showing than those in any other major type of institution. (See Table 8.) The small gap that separates average scores attained by students in the private universities from those in state universities and liberal arts colleges is significant at the 5 percent level.[9] The superiority of the private universities to the complex colleges and the teachers colleges is significant at the 1 percent level. A significant difference at this level also appears between the performance of students in private univer-

Table 7. SCORES OF THREE GROUPS OF LIBERAL ARTS STUDENTS

Major Field	Number of Cases	Mean Scores		Range of Scores[a]
Social Sciences	116	52.2[a]	65.3[b]	21–74
Humanities	111	47.1[a]	58.9[b]	26–72
Natural Sciences	130	45.0[a]	56.3[b]	15–75
Summary	357[c]	48.0[a]	60.0[b]	15–75

[a] Average number of questions answered correctly.
[b] Average percent of questions answered correctly.
[c] Excluding liberal arts students majoring in international relations, pre-professional and vocational fields. Hence, the difference between this figure and the total of 581 cited in Table 6.

sities and state universities on the one hand, and teachers colleges on the other. The low ranking of the latter in this analysis corresponds to that of students in all education curricula, as shown in Table 6.

The relatively low scores of our sample of students from technical schools appear to be in conflict with the high scores achieved by students in engineering curricula as shown in Table 6. Actually no conflict is indicated, since in the group of 52 technical school seniors, 15 were enrolled in curricula other than engineering.

Table 8. COMPARISON OF SCORES BY TYPES OF INSTITUTIONS

Type of Institution	Number of Cases	Mean Scores		Range of Scores[a]
Private University	445	45.8[a]	57.3[b]	17–74
State University	689	44.2[a]	55.3[b]	15–77
Liberal Arts College	234	43.8[a]	54.8[b]	17–72
Technical School	52	42.7[a]	53.4[b]	20–72
Complex College	380	42.7[a]	53.4[b]	15–74
Teachers College	54	39.5[a]	49.4[b]	17–67

[a] Average number of questions answered correctly.
[b] Average percent of questions answered correctly.

ANALYSIS BY GEOGRAPHICAL REGIONS

From Table 9, it can be inferred that seniors who were enrolled in colleges in the New England, Middle Atlantic, and Pacific states knew more about foreign affairs than did the seniors enrolled in colleges located in the Mountain, South, Midwest, and Great Plains states.[10] There were no significant differences among the means for the New England, Middle Atlantic, and Pacific states. The seniors in colleges in the Great Plains averaged among the lowest. Yet, one young man in a university in Texas scored higher than any student in any region.

Table 9. COMPARISON OF SCORES BY
GEOGRAPHICAL REGIONS

Region	Number of Cases	Mean Scores		Range of Scores[a]
New England	153	46.8[a]	58.5[b]	21–73
Middle Atlantic	366	46.3[a]	57.9[b]	15–74
Pacific	136	45.8[a]	57.3[b]	19–72
Midwest	449	44.1[a]	55.1[b]	15–75
Mountain	193	42.2[a]	52.8[b]	16–74
South and Southeast	376	42.0[a]	52.5[b]	17–73
Great Plains	181	42.0[a]	52.5[b]	20–77

[a] Average number of questions answered correctly.
[b] Average percent of questions answered correctly.

MEN VS. WOMEN

Judging from the results of the test, men students know more about foreign affairs than women. The average score for the 1,321 men tested was 46 correct answers; 529 women averaged 39.[11] The greater interest in public affairs displayed by men may help to explain this difference. Men students, it seems, absorb more information from newspapers, radio and television programs, and other extracurricular sources.

DIFFICULT QUESTIONS

In a test of this sort, items which floored 60 percent of the examinees may be fairly described as difficult. Some of the questions involving knowledge of geography fell into this category. For example, in their answers to Question 4, seventy-three percent of the seniors showed that they had only a hazy idea of what countries border on the USSR. Most of them did not know that Yugoslavia and the Soviet Union have no common frontier. Ignorance of climatic conditions in widely separated regions was revealed in the answers to Question 23. Thirty percent of the seniors thought that hot, dry summers were typical of London. An even greater number, 33 percent, were unaware that summer in Rio de Janeiro corresponds with the winter season in the northern hemisphere. Question 37 described the savanna regions of the world and asked the students to select the group of nations in which savannas could be found. Only 18 percent correctly selected the option containing Argentina (the pampas), the Soviet Union (the steppes), and the United States (the prairies). In spite of a reference to "clearing the grass sod," 29 percent selected an option which included Egypt. Fifty-two percent thought that the lack of shelter of trees was characteristic of Burma.

Confusion regarding United States foreign policy was evident in the answers to Question 27. Given a quotation which stressed United States aid to underdeveloped areas, 27 percent of the seniors thought it referred to the Marshall Plan and only a third correctly identified it with the Point Four Program. In the same field, United States foreign policy, answers to Question 3 revealed surprising ignorance. More than a quarter of the seniors listed the role of the United States in the Suez crisis as a reason why this country has become a target for anti-Westernism.

Thirty-seven percent of the students, queried about the Uniting for Peace Resolution (Question 47), thought that it had instituted the United Nations Command in Korea. Only 27 percent chose the correct answer—a declaration that the General Assembly should consider a breach of the peace immediately, if the Security Council was unable to exercise its responsibilities.

Question 80 required students to rank the USSR, Western Europe, and the United States according to population, total output (gross national product), output of electric power, and steel production. Only 39 percent of the students were able to answer this question correctly. A substantial number (43 percent) thought that the USSR had surpassed Western Europe in both population and output.

EASY QUESTIONS

Twenty-two questions in the test were answered correctly by 70 percent or more of the seniors. They found Question 7 the easiest: 91 percent of the seniors knew that an American president had intervened in foreign affairs by dispatching military forces to Korea. On Question 43, eighty-five percent showed that they could locate the major rubber-producing areas on a map of the world. Answers to Question 36 revealed that a large proportion of the students (72 percent) understood the effects of changes in visible and invi ible items in the United States balance of payments. Seventy-nine per-cent knew the location of the Suez Canal (Question 71); 7 percent, however, confused its location with the Panama Canal and a few placed it at the Straits of Gibraltar.

EVALUATION

On technical grounds, the test proved satisfactory. The scores on the various questions, when submitted to statistical procedures, showed that the test had a high degree of reliability.[12] The scores also showed no evidence of random marking. The strength or efficacy of the test was shown, furthermore, in its ability to discriminate consistently among students in various curricula and in various types of institutions and regions.

What can be said of the substantive results? What conclusions can be drawn from students' performance? Is an average score of 44 questions correctly answered out of 80—55 percent—good or bad? The answer to this query can be found only in an examination of the principles which determined the make-up of the Test and the selection of the questions. They were not designed for specialists in international relations. (In fact, a group of 15 men and women professionally active in foreign affairs had no difficulty with them; their average score was 75 correct answers.) Instead, the target was the non-specialist. The distinguished citizens who served as an advisory panel were asked to submit questions which, in their opinion, a college graduate of average intelligence, not particularly interested in foreign affairs, should be able to answer. The fact that a representative sample of college seniors could barely answer half of the questions, to my mind, must be considered a poor performance. It confirms, I believe, the general opinions quoted in Chapter 1, viz. that with respect to foreign affairs the average college senior is inadequately prepared for the responsibilities of citizenship and for the full enjoyment of life as an educated person.

In the reproduction of the Test on Foreign Affairs, the order of the following sets of questions has been reversed: 16 and 17, 43 and 44. Grateful acknowledgement is made to the following publishers for permission to use the materials indicated in the Test on Foreign Affairs: *The Evening Bulletin* (Philadelphia) for the cartoon Gulliver, by Alexander; St. Petersburg (Fla.) *Times* for the cartoon ". . . Had so many children she didn't know what to do," by Ivey.

TEST ON FOREIGN AFFAIRS

The purpose of this test is to measure the knowledge of college seniors about foreign countries, problems of American foreign policy, and international relations in general. The test is not intended for the specialist, but rather for the typical senior who may be enrolled in any one of a variety of curricula, such as Education, Business, Engineering, or Liberal Arts. The test is one part of a study of undergraduate education in international relations.

You will be given all the time you require to complete the test, although it is expected that most students will need from sixty to ninety minutes.

You are to mark your answer to each question on the separate answer sheet which is enclosed in this booklet. When you have decided which one of the suggested answers is best for a question, blacken the corresponding space on your answer sheet. You do not need to use a special pencil, but make sure your marks are heavy and dark.

Please fill in all the information requested in the blanks on the answer sheet. This information and the results of the test are to be used for research purposes only and will be kept in complete confidence.

Directions: Each of the questions or incomplete statements below is followed by four suggested answers or completions. Select the one which is best in each case and then blacken the corresponding space on your answer sheet.

1. In which of the following pairs of nations is a communist state coupled with a moderate socialist state?

   (A) Rumania and the Soviet Union
   (B) Italy and Britain
   (C) China and Spain
   (D) Poland and Sweden

2. "This nation has taken the view that independence means freedom to choose its own course in world affairs. It has refused to join the regional defense organization for South east Asia headed by the United States, but it has demon-strated its determination to uphold democracy by joining the Commonwealth."

   The nation referred to above is

   (A) Australia   (B) Pakistan
   (C) India   (D) Burma

3. "In spite of the fact that the United States has been traditionally an anti-imperialist country, and that in the past we have strongly supported the demands of colonial peoples for independence, this country is often the target of anti-Westernism."

   Which of the following has contributed to this situation?

   (A) Our treatment of the Philippine peoples
   (B) Our traditionally close association with Great Britain and France
   (C) Our role during the Suez crisis of 1956
   (D) Our granting of statehood to Hawaii

4. Which of the following does NOT border on the Union of Soviet Socialist Republics?

   (A) Yugoslavia   (B) Iran
   (C) Turkey   (D) Afghanistan

Gulliver

5. Gulliver, in the above cartoon, most likely represents which of the following organs of the United Nations?

(A) The General Assembly
(B) The Secretariat
(C) The Security Council
(D) The International Court of Justice

6. "In his opinion, political self-rule was part and parcel of the struggle for social and economic equality. The gulf between the rich and the hungry millions had to be closed. For him, also, the means were everything; as the means, so the end. Force to accomplish a purpose, no matter how worthy, was repugnant."

The ideas expressed above are most closely identified with

(A) Mao Tse-tung
(B) Woodrow Wilson
(C) Franklin D. Roosevelt
(D) Mahatma Gandhi

7. In which of the following instances did an American president intervene by dispatching military forces?

(A) When the Hungarians revolted against a Soviet-dominated regime
(B) When the Japanese entered Manchuria
(C) When North Korean forces invaded South Korea

   (D) When the state of Israel was formed after
        the partition of Palestine

8. "The strong leader, whose own efforts had largely freed
   his country from the enemy yoke in the Second World
   War claimed that he, not the Kremlin or the Cominform,
   was the true Marxist. Cautiously, for he was still a communist and a dictator, the United States gave him economic and military assistance."

   The leader referred to above is

   (A) Tito   (B) Gomulka
    (C) Nasser   (D) Sukarno

9. Which of the following was the first to evolve a policy of
   self-government for its African colonies?

   (A) Belgium   (B) France
    (C) Great Britain   (D) Portugal

10. In respect to which of the following are elections of mem-
    bers to the British House of Commons and to the United
    States House of Representatives most similar?

    (A) The length of the election campaign
    (B) The cost and character of the election
         campaign
    (C) The number of other officials elected on
         the same ballot
    (D) The proportion of the total number of seats
         to be filled in any one election

11. "Its insularity, its dependence on trade, and its potential
    for becoming the manufacturer merchant for its contin-
    ental neighbors suggest a comparison with England."

    This statement is most applicable to which of the follow-
    ing nations?

    (A) The Philippines   (B) Cuba
     (C) Japan   (D) Ceylon

12. In which chronological order did the following events
    occur?

    I. The United States organized the North
Atlantic Treaty Organization.

   II. The United States joined the United
Nations.

 III. The United States enunciated the Truman
Doctrine.

 IV. The United States launched the Southeast
Asia Treaty Organization.

(A) I, II, IV, III   (B) II, III, I, IV
  (C) III, II, IV, I   (D) IV, I, II, III

13. International law is most similar to national law in that it

(A) is generally based upon long-established
     principles or practices
(B) is enforced by a well-defined police power
(C) has been set down in specific codes which
     are universally accepted as binding
(D) insures that violators will be brought to
     trial and punished

14. Which of the following has done the LEAST to develop its
African possessions economically and politically?

(A) Belgium   (B) Great Britain
 (C) Portugal   (D) France

15. The United States took an active part in initiating which
of the following?

(A) The European Free Trade Association
(B) The Organization of European Economic Cooperation
(C) The Coal and Steel Community
(D) The European Economic Community

16. "It is white, as well as black nationalism that is
important in this African country. However, the whites
are divided into two distinct national groups, a division
which dates back to the settlement of the country, and
they are often at odds with each other."

The country referred to above is

(A) Algeria (B) Kenya
 (C) Nigeria   (D) Union of South Africa

17. The approximate date for the above map is

   (A) 1870   (B) 1910   (C) 1930   (D) 1950

18. "This nation is tightening its belt, encouraging free
   enterprise and seeking foreign capital in an attempt to
   emerge from the mess in which it was left by its former
   dictator. It wants continued financial backing by the
   United States, help in getting military equipment,
   and less competition from United States farm products
   in export markets."

   The nation referred to above is

   (A) Argentina   (B) Brazil
   (C) Chile   (D) Venezuela

19. "A free, open-minded, and absolutely impartial adjustment of all colonial claims, based upon a strict observ-
   ance of the principle that in determining all such questions of sovereignty the interests of the populations concerned must have equal weight with the equitable claims
   of the government whose title is to be determined."

   This quotation is part of

   (A) the Versailles Treaty
   (B) the Open Door Policy

(C) the Kellogg-Briand Pact
(D) Wilson's Fourteen Points

20. "Since the Spanish-American War these two former
Spanish colonies have pursued notably different courses.
One remained under American governors until after the
Second World War when it became a self-governing and
United States-associated state. The other quickly be
came sovereign and, with and without United States ass
istance, has gone from dictator to dictator and from rev-
olution to revolution."

Which of the following are referred to above?

(A) The Virgin Islands and Mexico
(B) The Hawaiian Islands and Panama
(C) The Philippine Islands and Haiti
(D) Puerto Rico and Cuba

21. "The aim of statesmen pursuing this policy was, generally, to preserve their own independence of action to the
utmost. Hence, the basic rule was to ally against any
state threatening domination. If one state seemed to dic
tate too much, others would shun alliances with it, unless
they were willing to become its puppets."

This policy is generally referred to as

(A) balance of power   (B) imperialism
 (C) isolationism   (D) co-existence

22. Some observers of the international scene have applied
the term "Balkanization" to developments in Africa today. The term is derived from the

(A) emergence of small independent states in
southeast Europe immediately before the
First World War
(B) efforts of the Balkan states to avoid involve-
ment in the Cold War
(C) drive of the Ottoman Turks to control the
Balkan peninsula in the nineteenth
century
(D) German Drang nach Osten of the late
nineteenth and early twentieth century

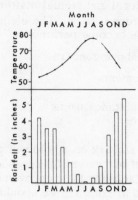

23. Which of the following places most probably has the type of climate characterized by the above graph?

   (A) London   (B) Chicago
   (C) Algiers   (D) Rio de Janeiro

24. Beginning with the earliest, which is the correct chronological order of the following?

   I. The abdication of King Farouk
   II The formation of the United Arab Republic
   III. The creation of the state of Israel
   IV. The Egyptian nationalization of the Suez Canal

   (A) I, III, II, IV   (B) III, I, IV, II
   (C) III, IV, I, II   (D) IV, II, I, III

25. Which of the following still retains a nominal political tie with the power which formerly controlled it?

   (A) Ethiopia with Italy
   (B) Ghana with Great Britain
   (C) The Philippines with the United States
   (D) Morocco with France

26. "One need only note the bitter controversy that still rages in the United States in relation to the regime which came to power in China in 1949 to realize that this issue

is no longer the purely legal and factual matter the government used to consider it to be. The element of approval-disapproval has become paramount."

The "issue" referred to above concerns

(A) bilateral trade agreements
(B) immigration policy
(C) foreign economic assistance pacts
(D) diplomatic recognition

27. "The United States must embark on a bold new program for making the benefits of our scientific advances and industrial progress available for the improvement and growth of underdeveloped areas . . . we should make available to peace-loving peoples the benefits of our store of technical knowledge in order to help them realize their aspirations for a better life."

The program referred to above is commonly known as the

(A) Marshall Plan
(B) Good Neighbor Policy
(C) Truman Doctrine
(D) Point Four Program

28. The shading on the map above represents

(A) mineral resources
(B) average annual rainfall
(C) major ethnolinguistic groups
(D) industrial resources

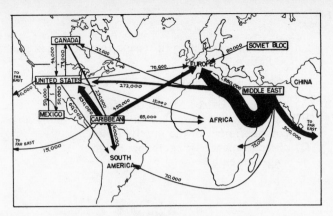

29. Which of the following is shown on the above map?

    (A) Major shipments of petroleum and
        petroleum products
    (B) Tonnage of major maritime powers
    (C) Major imports of raw materials
    (D) Imports and exports of major trading
        nations

30. In reference to which of the following have the United
States and the Soviet Union taken a similar position?

    (A) The suspension of nuclear tests
    (B) The United Nations inquiry into Hungarian
        revolt
    (C) The Anglo-French seizure of the Suez Canal
    (D) The unification of East and West Germany

31. "Since 1947 close to 400 million people speaking fourteen major languages have been knit into a single nation
of national consciousness previously unknown. A mixed
voluntary economy, directed by the central government
under a series of five-year plans, is being developed."

The leader of the nation referred to above is

    (A) Jawaharlal Nehru
    (B) Mao Tse-tung
    (C) Nikita Khrushchev
    (D) Juscelino Kubitschek

32. "Faced with this situation, many nations after the
Second World War felt compelled to discriminate
against imports from the United States at the same

time that they sought to increase their exports to the United States."

The situation referred to above was the

(A) raising of United States tariffs
(B) emergence of a "dollar gap"
(C) establishment of the sterling bloc
(D) discontinuance of reciprocal trade agreements

Low
Medium
High

33. The shading on the above map is used to indicate

(A) population density
(B) percentage of total labor force in agriculture
(C) per capita income
(D) death rate per thousand of population

34. Beginning with the earliest, which is the correct chronological order of the following?

  I. Stalin comes to power.
 II. The First World War ends.
III. The United States gives diplomatic recognition to the Soviet Union.
 IV. Nazi-Soviet Nonaggression Pact is signed.

(A) I, II, III, IV   (B) II, I, III, IV
(C) II, IV, III, I   (D) III, II, IV, I

35. "Emerging dazedly from the chaos of the Second World War, it was the most important political creed in Europe. Since then the tide has ebbed. Although its eclipse is a result of a variety of reasons, many of which apply only to specific countries, three general factors emerge. First, its liquidation by Communism in eastern Europe. Second, the change in the western European economic situation since 1949. Third, the lack of dynamic leadership."

Which of the following is referred to above?

(A) Stalinism   (B) Fascism
(C) Capitalism   (D) Socialism

36. "The United States has a trade surplus of 3 billion dollars a year, but that is not enough to cover military expenditures and other payments abroad amounting to 7.5 billion dollars a year."

The imbalance of 4.5 billion dollars could be reduced if there were an increase in

(A) exports of consumer goods
(B) expenditures of American tourists abroad
(C) imports of raw materials
(D) income from American investments by foreigners

37. "In all these regions of the world the experience of man in his attempt to form permanent fixed settlements has been similar. In a general way there are the same problems of securing water, of clearing the grass sod, of combating insect pests, and of building houses to withstand the extremes of weather in a land without the shelter of trees or hills."

The regions described above can most typically be found in which of the following groups of countries?

(A) Egypt, India, Mexico
(B) France, Germany, Italy
(C) Argentina, the Soviet Union, the United States
(D) Algeria, Burma, Saudi Arabia

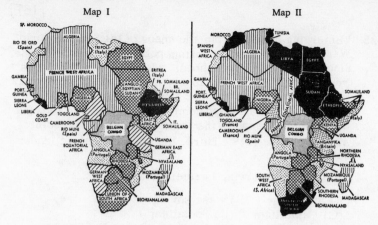

Map I   Map II

38. What are the most appropriate dates for Map I and Map II ?

(A) Map I: 1840; Map II: 1946
(B) Map I: 1879; Map II: 1935
(C) Map I: 1914; Map II: 1957
(D) Map I: 1932; Map II: 1950

39. The black areas on Map I and Map II represent

(A) the countries that are most industrially advanced
(B) British dominions
(C) independent countries
(D) Muslim countries

Country	Approximate Per Cent of Total World Production
Malaya	34
Indonesia	16
Bolivia	15
Thailand	7
China	6
Nigeria	5
Belgian Congo	4
Burma	3

40. Which of the following commodities is shown in the above table?

(A) Rice   (B) Copper   (C) Jute   (D) Tin

41. The increase in the membership of the United Nations from fifty nations in 1945 to over eighty in 1960 has resulted in a corresponding increase in the

(A) exercise of the veto power
(B) importance of the uncommitted nations
(C) influence of the big powers
(D) membership of the Security Council

42. Beginning with the earliest, which is the correct chronological order of the following?

I. Japanese seizure of Manchuria
II. Proclamation of the People's Republic of China (Communist China)
III. The Boxer Rebellion
IV. Establishment of the Kuomintang

(A) I, III, II, IV   (B) III, I, II, IV
(C) III, IV, I, II   (D) IV, I, III, II

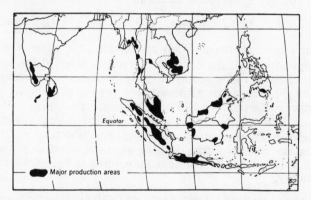

Major production areas

43. The above map would be used to show the chief world production areas for

(A) natural rubber   (B) coffee
(C) cotton   (D) iron ore

44. "These nations face similar problems—how to raise two blades of grass where one grew before, how to create industries for an area's untapped resources, and how to introduce basic social reforms without recourse to

strong-arm methods."

The above statement is most applicable to
which of the following groups of nations?

(A) Cuba, Spain, Yugoslavia
(B) Ghana, Indonesia, Israel
(C) Australia, Saudi Arabia, Poland
(D) Canada, Venezuela, Sweden

45. "The 1959 threat to the sovereignty of this country was
not as new as the newspaper headlines suggested. It
dates back to 1945 and was inspired and directed by Ho
Chi-minh. The communist offensive made considerable
head way in the last years before the nation received
its independence. Between 1954 and 1958 the communist cause was helped by apathy within the country and by
a Western effort that failed to achieve its basic objectives."

The country referred to above is

(A) Laos　　(B) Indonesia　(C) Burma　　(D) Taiwan

46. "The interdependence of all production processes is so
complicated that the desired balance between different
branches of the economy can, in the absence of a true
pricing process, be achieved only very gradually by a
cumbersome trial-and-error process. The financial
balances which finally emerge are of a technical rather
than an economic nature, and the prices which appear in
them are an accounting device, where dissimilar things
have to be added up, but have no guiding influence on the
economy."

The above quotation represents an evaluation
of the economy of

(A) West Germany　　(B) the Soviet Union
(C) Brazil　　(D) Italy

47. The "Uniting for Peace" resolution of the Fifth General
Assembly of the United Nations

(A) established a corps of United Nations
troops stationed in Geneva

(B) instituted the United Nations Command of
    troops in Korea
(C) requested the Secretary-General to exer-
    cise "quiet diplomacy" to effect an
    agreement among the big powers
(D) declared that the General Assembly should
    consider a breach of peace immediately
    if the Security Council was unable to
    exercise its responsibilities

48. Beginning with the earliest, which is the correct
    chronological order of the following?

    I.   The Yalta agreement
    II. The Potsdam agreement
    III. The Berlin blockade
    IV. The admission of the Federal Republic
         of Germany to NATO

    (A) I, II, III, IV   (B) I, III, IV, II
    (C) II, I, III, IV   (D) II, I, IV, III

    _____1957_____

China	41.4
France	18.5
Ireland	21.5
Japan	17.2
United States	25.3

49. Each of the above figures represents the

    (A) percentage of government budget devoted
        to military spending
    (B) birth rate per thousand of population
    (C) percentage of population which is illiterate
    (D) percentage of total food supply which is
        imported

50. In the twentieth century the situation illustrated by the
    cartoon has pertained most often to which of the follow-
    ing countries?

    (A) France   (B) Spain   (C) Canada   (D) India

"... Had so many children she didn't know what to do ..."

51. Which of the following best explains why Soviet technological achievements are of particular interest to those
areas caught up in the so-called revolution of rising expectations—the surge for both political independence
and economic advancement?

(A) Soviet technological achievements were
effected in spite of a Soviet population
explosion.

(B) Soviet technological achievements were
developed at little cost to the standard
of living.

(C) Soviet technological achievements have
been attained by a country that was only
recently considered underdeveloped.

(D) Soviet technological achievements were
brought about without recourse to
imperialistic practices.

52. Of the following, the policy of the United States government toward the Soviet Union may best be described as
one of

(A) interventionism   (B) conciliation
(C) containment   (D) passive resistance

53. Beginning with the earliest, which is the correct chrono-

logical order of the following?

I. The Italian invasion of Ethiopia
II. The Munich Conference on Czechoslovakia
III. The German invasion of Poland
IV. The establishment of the Vichy govern ment in France

(A) I, II, III, IV   (B) II, III, I, IV
(C) IV, I, III, II   (D) IV, III, II, I

54. "We would consider it intervention in the internal affairs of an American state if any power, whether by invasion, coercion, or subversion, succeeded in denying freedom of choice to the people of any of our sister republics."

In this pronouncement President Eisenhower is adding a new dimension to the

(A) Atlantic Charter   (B) Monroe Doctrine
(C) Open Door Policy   (D) Truman Doctrine

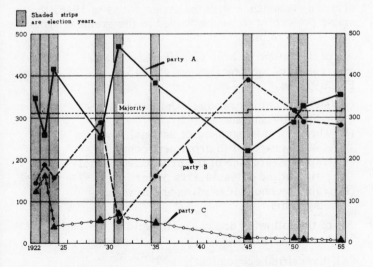

55. The graph above represents the political composition from 1922 to 1955 of which of the following?
(A) German Bundestag   (B) French National Assembly

(C)Italian Chamber of Deputies (D) British House of
Commons

56. It has been said that the French have never digested the
Revolution of 1789. Which of the following problems facing twentieth-century France is LEAST attributable to
this situation?

(A) The relation of church and state
(B) The relation between the executive and
the legislative
(C) The relation between the civilian and the
military
(D) The relation between the colonies and
metropolitan France

57. All of the following are members of the United Nations
EXCEPT
(A) Switzerland· (B) Hungary (C) Japan (D) India

58. "Almost fifteen years have passed since the first successful explosion of an atomic bomb. Instead of moving
toward disarmament or even controlled regulation of
arms in consonance with the expectations of 1945, the
major powers have been involved in the greatest arms
race known to man."

All of the following have contributed to the
frustration of the expectations of 1945
EXCEPT the

(A) serious deterioration in United States—
Soviet relations
(B) threat of infringement of national sover-
eignty entailed in armament control
(C) rapid resurgence of the productive capaci-
ties of the defeated Axis powers
(D) rapid technological advances in weapons
systems

59. All of the following are characteristic of the nations of
Southeast Asia EXCEPT

(A) diversified economies
(B) low per capita gross national product
(C) large Chinese populations
(D) a wealth of natural resources

60 All of the following are true about Canada's contemporary economic situation EXCEPT

(A) over one-half of Canada's foreign trade is
with the United States
(B) Canada's low wage scales continue to provide it with a strong competitive edge in
the world market
(C) Canada is dependent on foreign capital for
its industrial expansion
(D) Canada is one of the world's leaders in the
production and export of nonferrous
metals

61. "The chief threat today of outside interference in the
western hemisphere comes in a form never contemplat-
ed by the Monroe Doctrine. It is a threat of the spread
of communist doctrine aided by propaganda originating
in Moscow."

All of the following contribute to the gravity of this
threat EXCEPT the

(A) economic backwardness of Latin America
(B) political instability of Latin American
governments
(C) low priority given for loans and grants to
Latin America by the United States
(D) policy of nonintervention in the internal
affairs of other American republics by
the United States

62. In the twentieth century each of the following has been an
important geographic subject of controversy between the
nations listed after it EXCEPT
(A) the Saar—France, Germany
(B) the Nile River—Israel, Egypt
(C) the Indus River—Pakistan, India
(D) the Dardanelles—Turkey, the Soviet Union

63. All of the following have been partitioned as a result of
conflict between communist and non-communist powers
EXCEPT
(A) Korea (B) Vietnam (C) Germany (D) Palestine

64. All of the following are true of both the United States Congress and the United Nations General Assembly EXCEPT

   (A) individual members often align themselves in loosely organized blocs
   (B) each provides a forum for debate
   (C) each must approve the admission of new states
   (D) each has power to enact laws

65. In connection with either the First World War or the Second World War, the United States did each of the following EXCEPT

   (A) join a postwar organization to maintain peace
   (B) place limitations on freedom of speech and press
   (C) formally declare war on its enemies
   (D) join with its wartime allies in concluding a treaty of peace with Germany

66. The European powers have been interested in the Middle East for all of the following reasons EXCEPT:

   (A) The Middle East is the spiritual focal point for three of the world's great religions.
   (B) The Middle East is estimated to contain about fifty per cent of the world's known reserves of crude oil.
   (C) The Middle East has under cultivation only a small portion of its potentially arable land.
   (D) The Middle East is astride the most important single trade route between Europe and Asia.

67. Each of the following powers is correctly paired with the branch of the United States government which exercises it EXCEPT

   (A) declaration of war—the president

(B) approval of treaties—the Senate
(C) appointment of ambassadors—the president
(D) regulation of foreign commerce—Congress

68. "When a group or a party is in power it is under an obligation to fortify itself and defend itself against all
comers. The truth evident to all who are not warped by
dogmatism is that men have tired of liberty. They have
made an orgy of it. Liberty is today no longer the chaste
and austere virgin for whom the generations of the first
half of the nineteenth century fought and died. For the
gallant, restless, and bitter youth who face the dawn of a
new history there are other words that exercise a far
greater fascination, and those words are: order, hier-
archy, discipline."

The above statement could be representative of
the thinking of any of the following EXCEPT

(A) Mussolini   (B) Sun Yat-sen
 (C) Franco   (D) Petain

Directions: Below is a map of the world which has been
divided into squares numbered horizontally from 1 to 10 and
lettered vertically from A to F to enable you to locate places
more rapidly. For each of the questions which follow, select
the square which best answers the question and blacken the
space beneath the corresponding letter on the answer sheet.

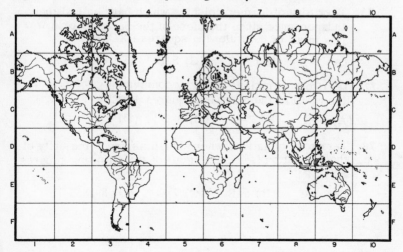

[178]

69. On this Mercator projection, land in which of the following squares is most exaggerated in size?

    (A) 2-C   (B) 4-E   (C) 5-D   (D) 8-A

70. The equator runs through which of the following squares?

    (A) 3-E   (B) 3-F   (C) 7-D   (D) 8-C

71. The Suez Canal lies in

    (A) 3-D   (B) 5-C   (C) 6-C   (D) 6-D

72. Formosa is located in which of the following squares?

    (A) 7-D   (B) 8-D   (C) 9-C   (D) 9-D

73. The Ural Mountains are in

    (A) 5-C   (B) 6-D   (C) 7-B   (D) 8-C

74. Territory which is part of the British Commonwealth of Nations lies in all of the following squares EXCEPT

    (A) 3-C   (B) 4-B   (C) 7-D   (D) 9-E

75. All of the following squares contain territory of member nations of the North Atlantic Treaty Organization EXCEPT

    (A) 4-E   (B) 5-B   (C) 5-C   (D) 6-C

76. Territory of former colonies which have gained their independence since the close of the Second World War lies in all of the following squares EXCEPT

    (A) 3-D   (B) 5-C   (C) 5-D   (D) 8-D

77. Territory of nations ruled by communist governments lies in all of the following squares EXCEPT

    (A) 6-C   (B) 7-D   (C) 8-D   (D) 9-C

78. Territory of nations where Muslims are a majority of the population is located in all of the following squares EXCEPT

    (A) 6-C   (B) 6-E   (C) 7-D   (D) 8-D

79. Territory of members of the Southeast Asia Treaty Organization can be found in all of the following squares EXCEPT

   (A) 5-C   (B) 8-D   (C) 9-C   (D) 9-E

80.   Using the blank spaces provided below, rank the United States, Western Europe, and the Soviet Union in terms of each of the four categories listed on the left. For each category assign a score of 3 to the area which ranks first, a score of 2 to the area which ranks second, and a score of 1 to the area which ranks third. When you have ranked the areas in terms of each of the four categories, total the scores assigned to each of the areas. From the options A-D below, select the answer which best ranks the areas from highest to lowest in terms of total score.

	United States	Western Europe*	Soviet Union
1. Population			
2. Total Output (Gross National Product)			
3. Electric-Power Output			
4. Steel Production			
Total			

   *Western Europe includes Austria, Belgium, Denmark, France, West Germany, Italy, Luxembourg, Netherlands, Norway, Sweden, Switzerland, Portugal and United Kingdom.

   (A) United States, Western Europe, Soviet Union
   (B) United States, Soviet Union, Western Europe
   (C) Western Europe, United States, Soviet Union
   (D) Soviet Union, United States, Western Europe

Appendix B. Institutions Which Participated in the Test

Institution	Schools Within Institutions				Classification	
	Business	Education	Engineering	Liberal Arts	Type[a]	Geographic Region
University of Alabama	x	x			State	South
Albion College				x	Lib. Arts	Midwest
American University				x	Complex	South
University of Arizona	x	x		x	State	Mountain
Arizona State University	x	x		x	Complex	Mountain
University of Arkansas	x	x			State	South
Arkansas Polytechnic College		x	x	x	Lib. Arts	South
Augustana College				x	Lib. Arts	Great Plains
Ball State Teachers College					Teacher	Midwest
Birmingham Southern College		x		x	Lib. Arts	South
Bowdoin College				x	Lib. Arts	New England
Bradley University	x	x	x	x	Complex	Midwest
University of Bridgeport	x	x	x	x	Complex	New England
Brigham Young University		x	x	x	Complex	Mountain
Brooklyn College				x	Complex	Middle Atlantic
Brown University				x	Private	New England
Bucknell University				x	Complex	Middle Atlantic

Institution					Region
University of Buffalo	x	x		Private	Middle Atlantic
University of California	x		x	State	Pacific
Carleton College				Lib. Arts	Midwest
Carnegie Institute of Technology			x	Tech.	Middle Atlantic
Centenary College			x	Lib. Arts	South
Central Connecticut State College	x	x		Teacher	New England
Central Missouri State College	x	x		Complex	South
Chatham College			x	Lib. Arts	Middle Atlantic
University of Chattanooga	x		x	Complex	South
University of Cincinnati	x	x^b	x	State	Midwest
Colby College			x	Lib. Arts	New England
Colorado College			x^b	Lib. Arts	Mountain
Colorado State University	x	x		Complex	Mountain
Columbia University	x			Private	Middle Atlantic
University of Connecticut	x			State	New England
Cornell University	x		x	Private	Middle Atlantic
Dartmouth College			x	Lib. Arts	New England
University of Delaware	x	x	x	State	Middle Atlantic
Denison University			x	Lib. Arts	Midwest
University of Denver	x	x	x	Private	Mountain
DePauw University			x	Lib. Arts	Midwest
University of Detroit	x			Private	Midwest

Appendix B. INSTITUTIONS WHICH PARTICIPATED IN THE TEST (Continued)

Institution	Schools Within Institutions				Classification	
	Business	Education	Engineering	Liberal Arts	Type[a]	Geographic Region
Drake University	x				Private	Midwest
Duke University			x		Private	South
Duquesne University	x	x			Private	Middle Atlantic
Earlham College				x	Lib. Arts	Midwest
Eastern Illinois University	x[b]	x			Complex	Midwest
East Tennessee State College	x[b]	x[b]			Complex	South
Emory University	x				Private	South
Evansville College				x	Lib. Arts	Midwest
University of Florida		x	x	x	State	South
Fordham University		x		x	Private	Middle Atlantic
Franklin Marshall College				x	Lib. Arts	Middle Atlantic
Furman University				x	Lib. Arts	South
University of Georgia	x	x		x	State	South
Gonzaga University	x		x		Complex	Pacific
Goucher College				x	Lib. Arts	Middle Atlantic

College					Type	Region
Grimel College				x	Lib. Arts	Midwest
Guilford College				x	Lib. Arts	South
Gustavus Adolphus College				x	Lib. Arts	Midwest
Hamilton College	x			x	Lib. Arts	Middle Atlantic
Hampton Institute			x	x	Tech.	South
Harvard University				x	Private	New England
Haverford College				x	Lib. Arts	Middle Atlantic
Hollins College				x	Lib. Arts	South
Hood College				x	Lib. Arts	Middle Atlantic
University of Houston	x			x	Complex	Great Plains
Howard College				x	Complex	South
Hunter College				x	Complex	Middle Atlantic
University of Idaho	x		x	x[b]	State	Mountain
Illinois College				x	Lib. Arts	Midwest
University of Illinois		x	x		State	Midwest
Indiana University		x[b]		x[b]	State	Midwest
State University of Iowa	x[b]	x[b]		x[b]	State	Midwest
Kalamazoo College				x	Lib. Arts	Midwest
University of Kansas	x	x		x	State	Great Plains
University of Kansas City	x			x	Private	Midwest
Kansas State Teachers College	x		x		Teacher	Great Plains

Appendix B. INSTITUTIONS WHICH PARTICIPATED IN THE TEST (Continued)

Institution	Schools Within Institutions				Classification	
	Business	Education	Engineering	Liberal Arts	Type[a]	Geographic Region
Kent State University		x			Complex	Midwest
University of Kentucky	x		x		State	South
Kenyon College				x	Lib. Arts	Midwest
Lafayette College				x	Complex	Middle Atlantic
Lehigh University	x			x	Private	Middle Atlantic
Lewis and Clark College				x	Lib. Arts	Pacific
Lindenwood College				x	Lib. Arts	Midwest
Louisiana State University				x	State	South
University of Maine		x	x		Complex	New England
Manhattan College	x		x	x	Complex	Middle Atlantic
Marquette University	x		x	x	Private	Midwest
Marshall College				x	Complex	Middle Atlantic
University of Maryland	x	x	x		State	Middle Atlantic
University of Massachusetts	x		x		Complex	New England
Massachusetts Institute of Technology			x		Tech.	New England
Miami University	x			x	Complex	Midwest

Institution	(1)	(2)	(3)	Type	Region
University of Miami	x	x		Private	South
University of Michigan	x	x	x	State	Midwest
Michigan State University	x	x	x	State	Midwest
Middlebury College			x[b]	Lib. Arts	New England
Millsaps College			x	Lib. Arts	South
University of Mississippi	x[b]	x[b]	x[b]	State	South
Mississippi Southern College	x	x	x	Complex	South
University of Missouri	x		x	State	South
Montana State University	x			State	Midwest
Montclair State College		x		Teacher	Mountain
Mount Holyoke			x	Lib. Arts	Middle Atlantic
					New England
University of Nebraska	x	x		State	Great Plains
University of Nevada	x		x	Complex	Mountain
University of New Mexico	x	x	x	State	Mountain
College of New Rochelle			x	Lib. Arts	Middle Atlantic
New York University	x	x	x	Private	Middle Atlantic
University of North Carolina			x	State	South
North Carolina State College		x[b]		Tech.	South
University of North Dakota	x[b]	x	x[b]	State	Great Plains
North Texas State College	x		x	Complex	Great Plains
Northwestern University	x	x	x	Private	Midwest
University of Notre Dame	x	x	x	Private	Midwest
Oberlin College			x	Lib. Arts	Midwest

Appendix B. INSTITUTIONS WHICH PARTICIPATED IN THE TEST (Continued)

Institution	Business	Education	Engineering	Liberal Arts	Type[a]	Geographic Region
Occidental College				x	Lib. Arts	Pacific
Ohio State University	x	x			State	Midwest
University of Oklahoma	x	x			State	Great Plains
University of Omaha	x	x			Complex	Great Plains
University of Oregon	x[b]	x		x[b]	State	Pacific
Pennsylvania State University	x	x[b]	x	x	State	Middle Atlantic
University of Pittsburgh		x		x	Private	Middle Atlantic
Pomona College				x	Lib. Arts	Pacific
Prairie View A & M College		x			Tech.	Great Plains
Princeton University				x	Private	Middle Atlantic
Rensselaer Polytechnic Institute			x		Tech.	Middle Atlantic
University of Rhode Island	x		x		State	New England
Rollins College				x	Lib. Arts	South
Roosevelt University	x			x	Complex	Midwest
Rutgers University			x	x	State	Middle Atlantic
College of St. Catherine				x	Lib. Arts	Midwest

Schools Within Institutions / *Classification*

Institution				Type	Region
Sacramento State College			x	Complex	Pacific
Saint Mary's University			x	Lib. Arts	Great Plains
University of San Francisco			x	Complex	Pacific
San Francisco State College	x	x	x	Complex	Pacific
San Jose State College	x	x	x	Complex	Pacific
Sarah Lawrence College			x	Lib. Arts	Middle Atlantic
Simpson College			x	Lib. Arts	Midwest
Smith College			x	Lib. Arts	New England
University of South Carolina	x	x	x	State	South
University of South Dakota	x	x	x	State	Great Plains
University of Southern California	x^b	x	x	Private	Pacific
Southern Methodist University	x	x	x	Private	Great Plains
Southwestern Louisiana Institute	x	x	x	Complex	South
Southwestern at Memphis			x	Lib. Arts	South
Stanford University	x	x	x	Private	Pacific
Stevens Institute of Technology		x	x	Tech.	Middle Atlantic
Syracuse University	x	x	x	Private	Middle Atlantic
University of Tennessee	x	x	x	State	South
University of Texas	x^b	x^b	x	State	Great Plains
Texas Christian University	x^b	x	x	Complex	Great Plains
Trenton State College		x		Teacher	Middle Atlantic
Tulane University	x	x		Private	South
Upsala College			x	Lib. Arts	Middle Atlantic

Appendix B. INSTITUTIONS WHICH PARTICIPATED IN THE TEST (Continued)

Institution	Schools Within Institutions				Classification	
	Business	Education	Engineering	Liberal Arts	Type[a]	Geographic Region
University of Utah		x			State	Mountain
Utah State University		x			State	Mountain
Valparaiso University				x	Complex	Midwest
Vanderbilt University				x	Private	South
University of Vermont		x			State	New England
University of Virginia		x	x	x	State	South
University of Washington	x	x	x[b]		State	Pacific
Washington State University	x	x			State	Pacific
Wayne State University	x	x		x	State	Midwest
Western Illinois University		x			Teacher	Midwest
Western Reserve University	x				Private	Midwest
Western Washington College		x		x	Teacher	Pacific
Westminster College				x	Complex	Midwest
West Virginia University		x		x	State	Middle Atlantic
Wheaton College				x	Lib. Arts	New England
Whittier College				x	Lib. Arts	Pacific
University of Wisconsin	x	x	x		State	Midwest

College of William & Mary		x	Lib. Arts	South
Wittenberg University		x	Lib. Arts	Midwest
Wofford College		x	Lib. Arts	South
University of Wyoming	x	x	State	Mountain
Yale University	x	x	Private	New England

[b] Indicates schools which participated in the test but whose answer sheets were received after the analysis had been undertaken.

[a] In assigning institutions to these categories, we have adopted the classification used by Natalie Rogoff in her study of College Board Members prepared for the College Entrance Examination Board.

Appendix C. Persons Who Submitted Suggestions for Test Questions

Dean Acheson
Frank Altschul
Marian Anderson
M. Margaret Ball
Marston Bates
James P. Baxter, 3rd
Marion W. Boggs
Frances P. Bolton
Robert R. Bowie
Frank H. Bowles
Robert F. Bradford
Harvie Branscomb
Harvey H. Bundy
McGeorge Bundy
Robert F. Byrnes
John C. Campbell
Oliver C. Carmichael
Marquis Childs
Benjamin V. Cohen
Henry S. Commager
James B. Conant
Arthur G. Coons
Joseph D. Coppock

Gardner Cowles
Vera M. Dean
John S. Dickey
William Diebold, Jr.
L. W. Douglas
Roscoe Drummond
James Terry Duce
Angus Dun
Mark F. Ethridge
A. Evans
Lawrence S. Finkelstein
Thomas K. Finletter
John Fischer
Manly Fleischmann
W. C. Foster
J. William Fulbright
Perrin C. Galpin
Harry D. Gideonse
A. J. Goodpaster
Heman Greenwood
Ernest A. Gross
William A. Hance
Joseph G. Harrison

Caryl P. Haskins
Francis H. Heller
Margaret Hickey
Mildred McAfee Horton
Bert F. Hoselitz
Hubert H. Humphrey
Jacob K. Javits
John K. Jessup
Joseph E. Johnson
Stephen B. Jones
Devereux C. Josephs
Milton Katz
Dexter M. Keezer
Grayson Kirk
Klaus Knorr
Francis J. Lally
Herbert Lewis
G. A. Lincoln
Herbert S. Little
Clare Boothe Luce
Flora B. Ludington
E. Wilson Lyon
William R. Mathews
E. W. McDiarmid
Gale W. McGee
Dempster McIntosh
Charles Merz
Walter Millis
George A. Morgan
Hans J. Morgenthau
Philip E. Mosely
Franklin D. Murphy
J. Morden Murphy
Edward G. Murray
Alfred C. Neal
Reinhold Niebuhr
Norman J. Padelford

Warren Lee Pierson
Sam Ragan
Clarence B. Randall
Mina Rees
G. Frederick Reinhardt
Winfield W. Riefler
James R. Roach
Walter Orr Roberts
Eleanor Roosevelt
Elihu Root, Jr.
Mrs. Oscar M. Ruebhausen
Dean Rusk
Francis H. Russell
John L. Simpson
David S. Smith
Lauren Soth
Leften Stavrianos
Richard P. Stebbins
Vilhjalmur Stefansson
Simon D. Strauss
Kenneth W. Thompson
Willard L. Thorp
Frank N. Trager
Arthur Upgren
Raymond Vernon
Eric A. Walker
James P. Warburg
B. B. Warfield
Albert C. F. Westphal
Howard P. Whidden
Francis O. Wilcox
Payson S. Wild
Anthony J. Wildman
Sidney Withington
A. Wolfers
Theodore P. Wright, Jr.
J. D. Zellerbach

In addition, suggestions from the following persons were received too late for consideration in framing the test:

Chester Bowles

William Marvel

David K. E. Bruce

C. Easton Rothwell

William A. M. Burden

Beardsley Ruml

Frank M. Coffin

Anna Lord Strauss

Dorothy Crook

Herman B. Wells

Frederick L. Deming

Gilbert F. White

Meyer Kestnbaum

Notes

Chapter 1. The Problem

1. *The Power of the Democratic Idea,* Special Studies Project Report VI, Rockefeller Brothers Fund, p. 66.

2. From an address to the Social Science Foundation, Denver University, February 24, 1958. Reprinted in John F. Kennedy's *The Strategy of Peace,* ed. by Allan Nevins (New York, Harper, 1960), p. 167.

3. Oscar Handlin, *John Dewey's Challenge to Education,* The John Dewey Society Lectureship Number Two (New York, Harper, 1959), p. 48.

4. Report of Discussions of Advisory Group at Northwestern University, April 12, 13, 14, 1956.

5. Random selection was obtained at each institution by application of a formula furnished by the Educational Testing Service.

Chapter 2. Neglected Opportunities

1. Summation of enrollments involves double counting, the same student having enrolled in several related courses. Hence, the actual number of students participating was considerably less than the total figures appear to indicate.

2. Classification according to geographical location or by type of institution proved impractical because of lack of sufficient transcripts in certain of the categories.

Except for engineering, transcripts from various types of institutions have been combined. Thus, the social science group includes students in state universities, private universities and liberal arts colleges. Likewise, the education group contains students with a major in education in liberal arts colleges, students in schools of education in state universities and students in teachers colleges. The business administration group is made up predominantly of students registered in state universities. In engineering, the contrast between the exposure of students in technical schools and those in state universities was so marked as to require separate statement.

Chapter 3. Foreign Affairs in General Education

1. *Higher Education for American Democracy: a Report of the President's Commission on Higher Education* (New York, Harper, 1948), pp. 48–49.

2. For a concise account of the present state of general education, see Algo D. Henderson's *Policies and Practices in Higher Education* (New York, Harper, 1960), pp. 113–28.

3. *35th Annual Confidential Guide to Lower Level Courses, 1960–61* (Cambridge, Mass., *The Harvard Crimson,* 1960), p. 29.

4. Justus Buchler, "Reconstruction in the Liberal Arts," in *A History of Columbia College on Morningside* (New York, Columbia University Press, 1954), p. 101.

5. Quoted from an article by Robert K. Webb in *Columbia College Today,* July, 1961, p. 7.

6. Charles C. Cole, Jr., "History in a General Education Program at Columbia College," *Journal of Higher Education,* October, 1956, p. 360.

7. Richard N. Swift, *World Affairs and the College Curriculum* (Washington, American Council on Education, 1959), pp. 57–58.

8. *1959–1960 Hunter College Bulletin, College of Arts and Sciences,* p. 106.

9. *Ibid.,* p. 107.

10. Paperbacks, mostly reprints of classic works, have been introduced in many courses to supplement, or even replace, the bulky textbooks that formerly held undisputed sway. The ultimate effects on higher education of making source material, and first-

rate monographs, available in this cheap and convenient form are not yet fully apparent. Some observers believe they will be revolutionary. See "The Paperback Textbook Revolution," by John Tebbel in *Saturday Review,* March 11, 1961.

11. Thomas H. Reed and Doris R. Reed, *Evaluation of Citizenship Training and Incentive in American Colleges and Universities* (New York, The Citizenship Clearing House, affiliated with the Law Center, New York University, 1950), pp. 14, 25.

12. *Goals for Political Science,* Report of the Committee for the Advancement of Teaching (New York, William Sloane Associates, 1951).

13. William M. Beaney, "The Introductory Course in Political Science," prepared for delivery at the 1958 annual meeting of the Political Science Association, St. Louis, Missouri, Sept. 4–6, 1958, p. 4 (mimeographed).

14. *Ibid.,* p. 2.

15. *Harvard Crimson, Confidential Guide,* 1960.

16. T. L. Carlson, "The Problem of Economic Illiteracy: A Preliminary Study," Western Michigan University, p. 7 (mimeographed).

17. Alonzo B. May, "The First Course in Economics," June, 1950 (mimeographed). Quoted in *The Teaching of Undergraduate Economics,* Report of a Committee of the American Economic Association, *American Economic Review,* Supplement, December, 1950, p. 1.

18. In one of the most popular texts, Samuelson's *Economics* (2d ed., New York, McGraw-Hill, 1951), five final chapters, five out of 35, 91 out of 746 pages, have these titles: "The Balance of International Payments," "Postwar International Economic Problems," "International Trade and the Theory of Comparative Advantage," "The Economics of Tariff Protection and Free Trade," and "Alternative Economic Systems." Bach's *Economics* (3d ed., Englewood Cliffs, N. J., Prentice-Hall, 1960), a close competitor, devotes six chapters, 120 pages in an 841-page book, to the same topics.

19. The J.C.E.E. is also cooperating with the National Task Force on Economic Education, appointed by the American Eco-

nomic Association, in a study designed to overhaul the teaching of economics in high school. "This makes economics the first of the social sciences to follow the revolutionary reforms instituted in mathematics and the [natural] sciences." For a description of the study, see the article by Fred M. Hechinger, The New York *Times,* March 6, 1961, which includes the sentence quoted above.

20. "Toward a Cultural Approach to Literature," *College English,* May, 1946, p. 459.

21. The three leading sociology textbooks are: William F. Ogburn and Meyer F. Nimkoff, *Sociology* (3d ed., Boston, Houghton Mifflin, 1958); Leonard Broom and Philip Selznik, *Sociology* (2d ed., Evanston, Ill., Row, Peterson and Company, 1958); and Arnod W. Green, *Sociology* (2d ed., New York, McGraw-Hill, 1956).

22. "Geography Almost Ignored in Colleges Survey Shows," The New York *Times,* December 18, 1950, p. 1.

23. J. R. Schwendeman, editor. Published by the Association of American Geographers, Southeastern Division, April, 1960, p. 1.

Chapter 4. Non-Western Civilizations

1. *Higher Education for American Democracy,* Report of The President's Commission on Higher Education (New York, Harper, 1947), Vol. I, p. 17.

2. *Asian Studies in Undergraduate and Teacher Education* (New York, Conference on Asian Affairs, Inc., 1955), p. 1 (mimeographed).

3. Quoted by Ward Morehouse in "Asian Studies in Undergraduate Education," *Journal of General Education,* July, 1958, p. 125.

4. "Regional Associates Survey of Non-Western Materials in the Undergraduate Curriculum," American Council of Learned Societies, *Newsletter,* January, 1961, p. 24.

5. In addition, there were small enrollments in courses in the geography of Russia and in the Russian language. See *The Non-Western Areas in Undergraduate Education in Indiana,* Robert F. Byrnes, editor. Indiana University Publications, Slavic and East European Series, Vol. XV, 1959, p. 12.

6. *Ibid.,* p. 26.

7. William Theodore De Bary, "Asian Studies for Undergradu-

ates," *Journal of Higher Education,* January, 1959, p. 3.

8. F. Champion Ward, "What *Did* Confucius Say?" *The Journal of General Education,* January, 1958, p. 3.

9. Robert I. Crane, "The Role of the Introductory Asia Course in Undergraduate Education," *The Journal of General Education,* July, 1959, p. 165.

10. Myron Weiner, "The Study of Indian Civilization at the University of Chicago: Needs and Choices," *Journal of General Education,* January, 1959, p. 26.

11. See *Asian Studies in Undergraduate and Teacher Education,* p. 10 and references there given.

12. *At Denison* (Granville, Ohio), November, 1959, p. 1.

13. Address of Dr. Charles F. Phillips, President, Bates College, at the Convocation of the College, September 24, 1959.

14. Marshall Hodgson, "A Non-Western Civilization Course in a Liberal Education . . . ," *The Journal of General Education,* January, 1959, pp. 43–44.

15. "What Should Be the Role of Area Programs in the 60's?" In Proceedings of the National Conference on Higher Education, Chicago, March 6–9, 1960, p. 193.

16. Urban Whitaker, "An Application of Area Studies to the Teaching of General Education Courses in International Relations," *International Review of Education* (Hamburg, Federal Republic of Germany), Vol. IV, 1959, pp. 425–40.

17. The February 1961 issue of the Newsletter of the Association of Asian Studies lists 32 summer programs in Asian studies for teachers to be held in 1961.

Chapter 5. Courses in International Relations

1. See "The Teaching of International Relations in the United States" by William T. R. Fox and Annette Baker Fox in *World Politics,* April, 1961, pp. 340–41.

2. Richard N. Swift, *World Affairs and the College Curriculum* (Washington, D.C., American Council on Education, 1959), pp. 118–19.

3. Fox, cited, p. 349.

4. Jennings B. Sanders, *Methods Used by College Social Science*

Departments to Improve Students' Understanding of Post-World War II International Tensions, Circular Number 362, U.S. Office of Education, December, 1952, p. 5.

Chapter 6. Professors in Uniform

1. See Hanson Baldwin's article on the ROTC, the second of a series of four, The New York *Times,* August 23, 1960.

2. Gene M. Lyons and John W. Masland, *Education and Military Leadership* (Princeton, N. J., Princeton University Press, 1959), p. 175. In the following paragraphs I have drawn freely from this excellent monograph.

3. *The United States and World Sea Power,* E. B. Potter, editor (Englewood Cliffs, N. J., Prentice-Hall, 1955).

4. *The Uniform on the Campus* (Columbus, Ohio, The Ohio State University, 1960), p. 28.

5. *Ibid.,* pp. 28, 29.

Chapter 7. Natural Sciences and the Humanities

1. Frederick L. Redefer, "The Care and Feeding of Provincials," *Saturday Review,* October 22, 1960.

2. Louise M. Rosenblatt, "Toward a Cultural Approach to Literature," *College English,* May, 1946, p. 460. See also Anna Balaikan, "The Integrated Approach to Literature," *School and Society,* October 12, 1957, pp. 279–80.

3. Harlan Cleveland, *The Overseas Americans* (New York, McGraw-Hill, 1960), p. 204.

4. Karl W. Deutch, "Toward an Inventory of Basic Trends and Patterns in Comparative and International Politics," *American Political Science Review,* March, 1960, p. 37.

5. See Publications of the Modern Language Association of America, September, 1959, and September, 1957. Degree requirements are evidence that college authorities believe some acquaintance with a foreign language should form "part of a student's intellectual baggage" when he leaves the campus, but for other purposes they are misleading. The fact that approximately 80 percent of all colleges and universities, enrolling an even larger proportion of the total undergraduate body, require language proficiency for B.A. and B.S. degrees does not tell us how many

students, at some time during their four-year course, actually are under instruction in language classes. Many institutions allow students to demonstrate proficiency in qualifying examinations. Others frequently waive the formal requirement to allow a student, deficient in languages but well-qualified in other studies, to get his degree.

6. For the text of the regulation and discussion, see *Modern Language Forum*, September–December, 1951, pp. 73–80.

7. PMLA, September, 1955, p. 53.

8. *The Overseas Americans*, p. 241.

9. The Act, in Title VI, authorized expenditures of $15¼ million in the fiscal year 1960 for "language development." Under this heading were included: (1) costs of operating on the college level language and area centers to train specialists in certain languages not commonly taught in this country; (2) payment of stipends to qualified individuals for advanced training in modern languages; and (3) costs of language institutes for advanced training of teachers in elementary and secondary schools.

On October 30, 1960, the U.S. Office of Education announced that it had invested $8,400,000 ". . . in the development of grammars, tape recordings . . . and other instructional materials" to promote the study of 83 "critical foreign languages and dialects, many of which are not now taught in any American college or university." New York *Herald Tribune*, October 31, 1960.

10. The data are taken from *Modern Language News*, published by Appleton-Century-Crofts, February, 1960. The number of reporting institutions has varied from about 500 to 700.

11. U. S. Department of Health, Education, and Welfare, *Guide to the National Defense Education Act of 1958*, by Theodore E. Carlson (Washington, Government Printing Office, 1960), p. 16.

12. "Developing Cultural Understanding through Foreign Language Study: A Report of the Modern Language Association Interdisciplinary Seminar in Language and Culture," PMLA, December, 1953, p. 1200.

13. *Ibid.*, p. 1201.

14. Henri Peyre, "The Need for Foreign Languages in America Today," Bulletin of the New England Modern Language Association, February, 1951, p. 10.

15. "The Purdue Language Program," by Elton Hocking in PMLA, September, 1955, p. 36.

16. *Ibid.*, p. 39.

Chapter 8. College Curricula

1. The following paragraphs have been adapted from the excellent descriptions in George P. Schmidt's *The Liberal Arts College* (New Brunswick, N. J., Rutgers University Press, 1957), pp. 209–10.

2. *Carleton College Bulletin*, March, 1959, pp. 119–21.

3. The Liberal Arts College, p. 211.

4. Harlan Cleveland, *The Overseas Americans* (New York, McGraw-Hill, 1960), p. 206.

5. The New York *Times*, May 15, 1960.

6. ACLS Newsletter, January, 1961, p. 15.

7. Joseph D. Coppock, "International and Foreign Affairs in a Liberal Arts College," *The Non-Western Areas in Undergraduate Education in Indiana*, ed. by Robert F. Byrnes. Vol. XV, Slavic and East European Series, Indiana University Publications (1959), p. 44.

8. *World Affairs and the College Curriculum*, p. 169. See also, pp. 103–6.

Chapter 9. Students and Faculty

1. Fred Cole, *International Relations in Institutions of Higher Education in the South* (Washington, D. C., American Council on Education, 1958), p. 18.

2. Dr. Rose K. Goldsen, *et al.*, *What College Students Think* (Princeton, N. J., D. Van Nostrand Company, 1960).

3. *Ibid.*, p. xxii.

4. *Ibid.*, p. 199.

5. Yale Alumni Magazine, June, 1960.

6. Earl J. McGrath, *The Graduate School and the Decline of Liberal Education* (New York, Teachers College, Columbia University, Bureau of Publications, 1959), p. 34.

7. *What College Students Think*, p. 7.

8. Karl Bigelow has remarked that, for many young people, general education is ". . . too placid an experience. . . . They go

through it like a case of measles, accepting it as a normal but not very significant aspect of life." In an address at a Boston University Junior College Conference on "Problems and Prospects in General Education." September 19–21, 1957, p. 73 (mimeographed).

9. *International Relations.* p. 147.

Chapter 10. *Summary and Recommendations*

1. "The College and University in International Affairs," Fifty-Fifth Annual Report of the Carnegie Foundation for the Advancement of Teaching, 1959–60, p. 14.

2. This is Harlan Cleveland's estimate. See *The Overseas Americans*, p. 206. In following pages he has provided useful information, and critical judgments, on foreign study programs.

3. "Young Americans Abroad," Carnegie Corporation of New York Quarterly, January, 1961, p. 1.

4. Fred Cole has suggested ". . . the need, if not in every institution, certainly in most institutions, for a person or persons who can serve as a focal point for assisting in the development of institution-wide planning for teaching nonspecializing students some basic knowledge about international relations." See *International Relations in Institutions of Higher Education in the South*, p. 148. This recommendation owes much to his suggestions.

Dean Hartzell of Bucknell University, in a letter to the author, has urged that a single faculty member should be designated to coordinate activities in undergraduate education in international relations, "with the specific purpose of reaching a larger segment of the student body." Columbia University's recently appointed Coordinator of International Studies, Mr. David S. Smith, is at present concerned only with relevant courses and programs in the various graduate schools of the University.

5. Quoted from an address by Wendell L. Willkie on "The Importance of Liberal Education Policies," Duke University, January 4, 1943. In *Vital Speeches*, Feb. 15, 1943, p. 261.

Appendix A. *A Test on Foreign Affairs*

1. The analysis of the data refers to only 1,854 cases; 104 papers were received too late for consideration.

2. In assigning institutions to these categories, we have adopted

the classification used by Natalie Rogoff in her study of College Board Members prepared for the College Entrance Examination Board.

3. The mean score (arithmetic average) was 44.0, with a standard deviation of 11.6. The median was 43.8; the upper quartile, 52.1; and the lower quartile, 35.5.

4. In this study, significant differences, unless otherwise noted, are those which might not occur by chance more than once in a hundred times.

5. Educational Testing Service, *Annual Report to the Board of Trustees 1951–52*, p. 14.

6. Frank C. Pierson and others, *The Education of American Businessmen* (New York: McGraw-Hill, 1959), p. 63. See also pp. 59–61; 65–69.

7. For the purpose of this study, liberal arts majors have been grouped under the following headings: *Social Sciences:* anthropology, economics, geography, history, political science, sociology; *Natural Sciences:* biology, chemistry, geology, mathematics, physics, psychology; *Humanities:* English, foreign languages, literature, philosophy, religion. The following liberal arts majors were omitted from this classification: international relations, pre-professional fields (e.g., pre-law, pre-medicine, art, music) and vocational fields (e.g., home economics, radio, speech).

8. The data for state and private universities, complex colleges and technical schools refer to students enrolled in any of the four curricula analyzed in Table 6. The data for liberal arts colleges refer only to seniors enrolled in a liberal arts curriculum. Likewise, only seniors enrolled in an education curriculum figure in the data given for teachers colleges.

9. I.e., this difference would not occur by chance more than five times in a hundred.

10. The high ranking of seniors in the New England, Middle Atlantic, and Pacific states is probably related to the selective admissions policies of institutions in those regions.

11. Four of the 1,854 students did not supply information regarding their sex.

12. Reliability is ordinarily expressed as a correlation coefficient. The coefficient for this test, as determined by the Kuder-Richardson formula, was .89.

Index